D0244509

FEMINISM
is...

04553197

FEMINISM is...

WRITTEN BY
ALEXANDRA BLACK
LAURA BULLER
EMILY HOYLE AND
DR MEGAN TODD

CONSULTANT
DR DEBRA FERREDAY

Senior Editors Scarlett O'Hara, Georgina Palffy
Senior Designer Sheila Collins
Editors Sarah Edwards, Anna Streiffert Limerick,
Sarah MacLeod, Vicky Richards, Jenny Sich
Designer Kit Lane
Illustration Sheila Collins, Kit Lane
Picture research Deepak Negi

Managing Editor Francesca Baines
Managing Art Editor Philip Letsu
Publishing Director Jonathan Metcalf
Associate Publishing Director Liz Wheeler
Art Director Karen Self
Producer, Pre-production Jacqueline Street
Senior Producer Angela Graef

Jacket Designers Tanya Mehrotra, Stephanie Cheng Hui Tan
Jacket Design Development Manager Sophia MTT
DTP Designer Rakesh Kumar
Jackets Editorial Coordinator Priyanka Sharma
Managing Jackets Editor Saloni Singh
Jacket Editor Emma Dawson

First published in Great Britain in 2019
by Dorling Kindersley Limited,
80 Strand, London WC2R 0RL

Copyright © 2019 Dorling Kindersley Limited
A Penguin Random House Company
2 4 6 8 10 9 7 5 3 1
001 – 259135 – Jan/2019

All rights reserved. No part of this publication may be reproduced, stored in a
retrieval system, or transmitted in any form or by any means, electronic,
mechanical, photocopying, recording, or otherwise, without the prior written
permission of the copyright owner.

A CIP catalogue record for this book is available from the British Library.
ISBN 978-0-2412-2802-9

Printed and bound in China.

A WORLD OF IDEAS:
SEE ALL THERE IS TO KNOW
www.dk.com

CONTENTS

FEMINISM is...

Feminism. The dictionary says it's the belief that men and women should be treated equally – politically, economically, and socially. It's not exactly the shortest statement to brandish across your chest on a T-shirt is it?

BUT, overall it sounds pretty reasonable, surely? So why are so many women – and men – nervous about calling themselves a feminist? They shouldn't be. In my opinion, it's a hopeful term to associate ourselves with – it means you believe in human rights, after all.

That's what this book is all about, breaking it down beyond a "statement T-shirt". It will help you to explore, unpick, and understand feminism and its story so far. This book in your hands right now and the words you're about to read shine a light on some of the extraordinary women who have made, and are making, feminism happen. The ideas are there to stimulate your mind and help you to ask your own questions, but what you take away from all this information is up to you. We all experience life under different circumstances, which shapes us into who we are, but understanding other people's stories and ideas is vital. Learning why people fight for feminism is empowering and reminds us that, though it's easy to get frustrated and engage in "click bait" and social media arguments, we all have a beating heart underneath. Learning to listen to different sides of arguments, understand ideas, and think about issues in a way you haven't before is important, and reading books is key to help us do this thoughtfully.

You are the future and you have the power to change things for the better – HOW EXCITING! You might not agree with everything you read – that's down to you – but think big and you will figure out what feels true to you. I hope you become as inspired by feminism as I have been.

Now go ... DIVE RIGHT IN.

Gemma Cairney

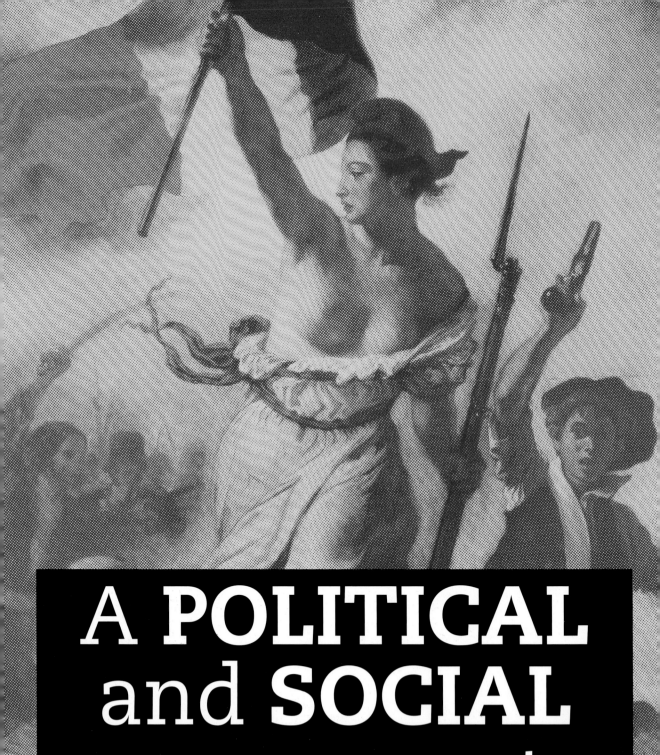

A **POLITICAL**
and **SOCIAL**
movement

What is FEMINISM?

Is it a MAN'S world?

The RIGHT to an EDUCATION

FIGHTING for a cause

VOTES for women!

WOMEN at war

(Un)Equal RIGHTS!

Women's LIBERATION

Living WITHOUT MEN

BACKLASH!

Girl POWER!

·Everyday SEXISM

#MeToo

Feminism is a movement that fights for change. Early feminists campaigned to end slavery, and for equal suffrage and human rights for women. Later feminists continued this progress, focusing on other inequalities affecting women, such as in education and relationships. Today, the movement is still powerful – calling out sexual harassment and addressing the sexism in everyday situations.

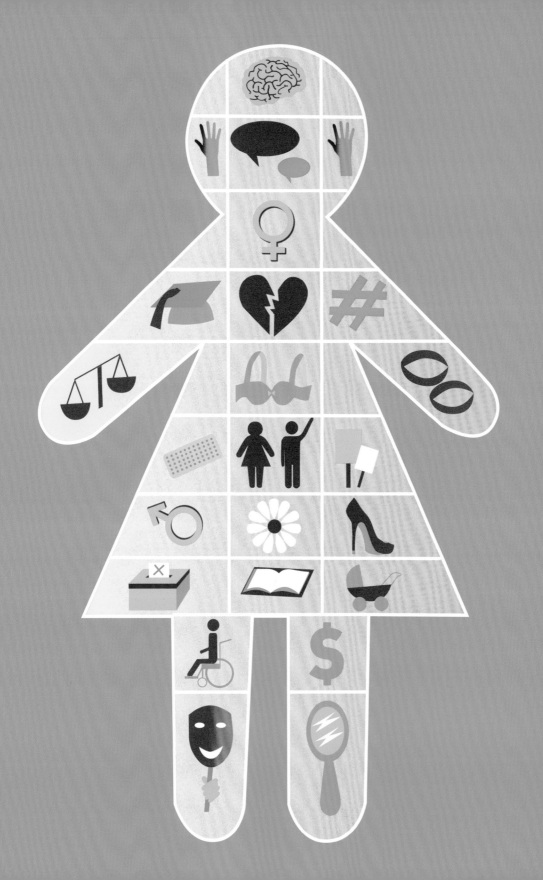

What is FEMINISM?

Most of us will have heard the word feminism but might struggle if someone asked us to explain it. What is feminism, and who is it for? It doesn't have to be complicated. As the UK campaign group the Fawcett Society has stated, "the simple truth is if you want a more equal society for women and men then you are in fact a feminist".

Challenging inequality

For every book about feminism there are probably as many definitions – its diversity is both its joy and challenge. Common to most definitions, however, is a belief that men and women, girls and boys, should be treated equally (and a recognition that, at the moment, we're not). It's not about arguing that men and women are the same, nor that all women are the same. It is a belief that despite our differences we should all be treated fairly and with respect. It is about equal rights and opportunities for all.

> **A US 2018 poll found that young women were more likely than young men to be active in politics.**

Feminist struggle

Feminism is about action. It is a movement that seeks to bring about positive social change. And it has been massively successful – transforming society at all levels. Many women across the globe now have the vote, a right to an education, and more representation in the media. But there's still a way to go. Although many of its goals have been set in motion – there are laws on equal pay, rape and domestic violence are crimes in many nations, divorce is more accessible – they have not all been achieved. Women in different parts of the world face different daily challenges, and, even in the developed world, poverty, hunger, illiteracy, and violence remain issues for some.

Celebrating difference

Feminist thinkers focus on the interplay of gender, race, disability, sexuality, class, and power to make sure feminism is relevant to us all. They see the shared aspects of women's experiences while being aware of difference – in identity, lived experience, and forms of privilege. And it's a myth that feminists think that women should have more power than men. In fact, the social change that feminists want would benefit all people, freeing both women and men from restrictive gender roles. Nigerian author Chimamanda Ngozi Adichie, in *We Should All Be Feminists* (2014), says "a feminist is a man or a woman who says, yes, there's a problem with gender as it is today and we must fix it, we must do better. All of us, women and men, must do better". A feminist is someone who fights for equality, who challenges prejudice, discrimination, and sexism. To be a feminist is something to be proud of!

> **"I'm a feminist. I've been a female for a long time now. It'd be stupid not to be on my own side."**
>
> **Maya Angelou (2014)**

Is it a **MAN's** world?

A central idea of feminism is that we are living in a patriarchy – a society that values men over women, and where men hold the power and women are largely excluded from it. So have the odds been stacked against women from the start?

The creation of patriarchy

Feminists have argued that human societies have historically been largely patriarchal. In *The Creation of Patriarchy* (1986), Austrian American feminist historian Gerda Lerner examined how males came to dominate over the course of history. She argued that this was not a natural state of affairs – a consequence of biological differences between men and women – but simply circumstantial. Her theory was that patriarchy emerged thousands of years ago, at the same time as the first cities were established, as a way of controlling reproduction so that men could be sure who their offspring were and property could be inherited through the male line.

MATRIARCHY

Feminist historians have speculated about whether societies that existed before recorded history might have been organized differently. Artefacts such as the 25,000-year-old Venus of Willendorf (right) have been interpreted by some as evidence that prehistoric cultures worshipped female gods and may even have been matriarchal – run by women.

Patriarchy today?

In a patriarchy, men have the power within the family, but also in society as a whole because the society's institutions, such as the media, law, education system, and religion, deny women access to power. These institutions also transmit the values of the state, helping to forge our ideas about the world. British feminist Sylvia Walby argues in *Theorizing Patriarchy* (1990) that there are six key "structures" that support patriarchy: the family household, paid work, politics, culture, violence, and attitudes towards sexuality. Even a brief look at some of these structures shows how inequalities persist. At work a legal right to equal pay has not erased the gender pay gap, and in the home women still do most of the chores. But other feminists have criticized the concept of patriarchy because it suggests that all men benefit equally from women's oppression. In fact, American feminist bell hooks argues that some men are more oppressed by the patriarchy than some women. She also says that women too have been socialized into sexist thought and action, so it is wrong for feminist thinkers to see feminism as simply being for all women against all men.

Changing times

Despite more than 100 years of the feminist movement, many would still argue that we are living in a world shaped by men, with women still running to catch up. In *End of*

Equality (2014), British feminist Beatrix Campbell argues that in our current global economy the patriarchy has been reborn in an era of "neopatriarchy", where increased social inequality and the patriarchy work together to oppress women. Campbell argues that women suffer the most from austerity (government policies to reduce spending on public services) because state welfare helps to alleviate women's poverty as a result of their unequal pay and unpaid work. Her theory is that just as feminism of the 20th century started to make an impact, patriarchal power has reasserted itself in new ways and progress has reversed. She says it will take a brand new revolution to achieve equality.

> "Men have been given the impression that they're much more important in the world than they actually are."
>
> Gerda Lerner (1994)

THE INSTITUTIONS THAT SHAPE AND RUN SOCIETY ARE THE PILLARS OF THE PATRIARCHY

The RIGHT to an EDUCATION

Education is a gateway to freedom, opportunities, and independence, and one through which both sexes should have the right to pass. We may associate feminist demands for equal education for girls and boys with the women's rights campaigners of the 19th century, but the battle has a longer history. In some countries, it is not yet won.

What chance of an education?

There are some historical examples of societies that did not question women's right to study. For instance, as early as the 8th century BCE, the ancient Greek city-state of Sparta allowed women and men equal access to education. From around 600 BCE, until approximately 500 BCE, girls in India had free access to education, too. However, such attitudes were not typical. For example the academies of ancient Athens rarely admitted women, and educated women such as Hypatia (c.355-415 CE), a mathematician, were the exception.

In medieval Europe, most children from the poorer classes received no education at all, starting work at a young age. Boys from privileged homes might have had a tutor, or attended grammar school. Girls from wealthy families had limited, if any, schooling. A girl's best chance of an education was in a convent. In fact, convents produced some of the great intellects of the Middle Ages, such as German philosopher and composer Hildegard von Bingen (1098–1179).

Demanding equal schooling

Women were by no means silent about being excluded from education. Italian Christine de Pisan (1364–c.1430) was one of the many who spoke up for women's right to study. Marie Le Jars de Gournay, a French writer, produced an important work, *Equality between Men and Women,* in 1622, in which she argued

FEMINISTS CAMPAIGNED FOR SCHOOLS TO OPEN THEIR DOORS TO GIRLS,

Once, only boys were considered worth sending to school.

that one of the reasons for women's lack of equality in society was that they were denied an education. In 1638, the German-born Dutch scholar Anna Maria van Shurman – a linguist, poet, artist, and engraver – insisted that women were suited to scholarly life. She became the first woman to study at university in Europe (although she had to sit behind a curtain during lectures).

Enlightening times

In the 18th century, the progressive European intellectual movement known as the Enlightenment, along with the French Revolution (1789–99), inspired women to campaign for their rights in a more organized way. At a time when many people were questioning the way societies were governed, women began to press for change based on principles of liberty and equality. French feminist Olympe de Gouges (1743–93) outlined the problems that come with no education in her pamphlet *Declaration of the Rights of Woman*

DIVIDED CLASSROOMS

In the early 20th century, girls had a more limited education than boys. Subjects such as maths and science, routinely studied by boys, were regarded as less appropriate for their female peers. A typical curriculum for girls focused on domestic arts such as housekeeping and needlework.

(1791). English philosopher and activist Mary Wollstonecraft stated in *A Vindication of the Rights of Woman* (1792) that schooling would give women the independence to take care of themselves. English intellectuals developed these views. These included Harriet Taylor Mill (1807–58), who thought education necessary for a woman's sanity, and Harriet Martineau (1802–76), who argued that women's inferiority was due to a lack of mental training.

By the early 20th century, girls in Western Europe and the US had by law to attend school at least until their early teens, but this was not the case the world over. Today, 15 million girls around the world will never go to school.

> ## "When girls are educated, their countries become... more prosperous."
>
> Michelle Obama (2013)

See also: 96–97, 98–99

AND SO THROW OPEN DOORS TO WIDER OPPORTUNITIES

Modern education gives girls equal opportunities.

FIGHTING for a cause

Until the late 18th century, women's opinions about how society and politics should work had rarely been heard, or taken into account. At this time, an abolitionist movement was growing, demanding the end of slavery. Within it, women began to speak out for increased women's rights, too.

Women against slavery

Since the 15th century, European nations, and later the Americas, had grown prosperous through the slave trade and the labour of enslaved men, women, and children taken forcibly from Africa. By the late 18th century, many people – men and women, black and white, freeborn and ex-slaves – were demanding the abolition of this barbaric practice. But many male abolitionists objected to female campaigners participating in their meetings. In the US, schoolteachers Sarah Mapps Douglass, a middle-class African American, and Lucretia Mott, a white Quaker, formed the Female Anti-Slavery Society in 1833. At their meetings, they often had to confront violent racists as well as disapproving men. At the first World Anti-Slavery Convention, held in London, UK, in 1840, Mott hoped to be invited to speak. Instead, together with abolitionist Elizabeth Cady Stanton, she was hustled behind a curtain, where they could listen to the men but be kept out of sight. Their frustration at such treatment led them to focus on the rights of women.

Declaration of independence

Stanton and others likened the plight of women to that of slaves – both were denied an education and the vote, engaged in unpaid labour, and regarded as a man's property, although this comparison overlooks the brutal violence slaves were subjected to. In 1848, Stanton, Mott, and others organized the first ever women's

FREEING HER PEOPLE

Harriet Tubman escaped from slavery in 1849, and then helped hundreds of runaway slaves escaping to the north and freedom through the secret network known as the Underground Railroad. She was also an activist for women's rights.

THE PROGRESS OF ANTI-SLAVERY CAMPAIGNERS LED THE WAY FOR WOMEN'S RIGHTS

rights conference, the Seneca Falls Convention. There they discussed issues affecting women, such as property laws, marriage, and education. Their closing statement, imitating the US Declaration of Independence, outlined the rights due to women. Many see this conference as the beginning of American first-wave feminism.

Susan B. Anthony, another abolitionist, joined forces with Elizabeth Cady Stanton in the 1850s. Together they founded several women's groups. Soon campaigners were raising awareness about inequality through magazines, protests, and talks.

Still not equal

Slavery was eventually abolished in the US in 1865. Many women felt they were now forced to choose between fighting for voting rights for all (black and white) or concentrating on female suffrage. Eventually, most American women were granted the right to vote in 1920.

However, the US was still not an equal nation, continuing to oppress black people, especially in the southern states. Women such as Rosa Parks, famous for refusing to give up her bus seat to a white man in Alabama in 1955, played an important role in the activism of the US civil rights movement. This movement achieved its main goal, at least in theory, when racial discrimination was declared illegal in the US in 1964 – but black women still had many rights left to fight for. The civil rights activism inspired other movements. A new culture of protest was developing – against capitalism, against the Vietnam war, against the establishment and the status quo. Feminists found a voice, too. By the 1960s and 1970s, women in many countries, not just the US, could see possibilities opening up. In what became known as second-wave feminism, they adopted many civil protest strategies to fight their cause.

See also: 22–23, 24–25, 58–63

"We Abolition Women are turning the world upside down."

Angelina Grimké, abolitionist (1838)

Sojourner Truth

c.1797–1883

The extraordinary story of Sojourner Truth made her campaign for the rights of women all the more persuasive. Born into slavery in the US, she escaped to freedom, aged around 30, after years of physical and emotional abuse. She went on to give influential speeches in support of all the issues she felt strongly about, often based on her own experiences: the abolition of slavery, women's suffrage, and the rights of freed black people to own land.

> **"...we'll have our rights; see if we don't; and you can't stop us from them; see if you can."**

She gave her most famous speech in 1851 at the Women's Rights Convention in Ohio. Short and simple, it questioned the view that women were weaker than men and therefore should not have the same rights. Truth challenged any doubters: "Look at me! Look at my arm! I have ploughed and planted, and gathered into barns... I could work as much and eat as much as a man – when I could get it – and bear the lash as well! And ain't I a woman?"

Ahead of her time

In 1828, Truth took a white man to court for illegally selling her son into slavery, and won – setting an example of how former slaves could assert their rights. She was not afraid of clashing with leading abolitionists as she argued for equal rights for women as well as for an end to slavery. Today she is seen as an influential trailblazer and, in 1997, NASA named a Mars rover in her honour.

Sometime ally
Truth first met the prominent abolitionist Frederick Douglass (1817–95) in the 1840s. He often spoke out in favour of women's rights, but later came to believe that it was more important to prioritize getting the vote for black men, rather than for women.

Against all odds

Born on a slave-owning estate in New York state, Truth was sold at an auction for the first time when she was only nine years old. She came to be sold another three times, was brutally beaten, and lost two of her children. In 1826, she "walked off to freedom" (her own description of her escape), a year before New York state freed slaves born before 1799.

"Ain't I a woman"

Truth never learnt how to read or write, but she knew what she believed in and was very good at formulating her thoughts.

Knowing her worth
Tall, charismatic, and confident, Truth was a popular speaker who could stand up both to racist mobs and male hecklers. She promoted herself through portraits like this one, taken in 1863.

VOTES for women!

Women today may take for granted their ability to play an active role in politics. But it took years of campaigning before women were granted suffrage – the right to vote – and were able to become involved in making and changing the laws that affected them.

The way it was
In the 19th century, women in most parts of the world were not allowed to vote. It was assumed that a woman's role was to take care of her family and the home, and most women had been brought up to believe that it was their husband's place to represent them when voting.

Awakening
With the Industrial Revolution, things started to change. Many more women were in full-time employment outside of the home, so they now had opportunities to meet in large organized groups to discuss political and social issues.

Britain was just one of the Western countries where campaigns for suffrage grew. In 1865, MP John Stuart Mill presented a Woman's Suffrage petition to Parliament, and women's groups soon sprang up to press the issue further – filled with women from varied social and ethnic backgrounds. Suffragists, led by Millicent Fawcett, used peaceful strategies to gain support. Suffragettes, led by Emmeline Pankhurst and her daughters, felt that law-breaking was needed to force the government to act. Their controversial methods (see pp 24–25) and the government's brutal response divided public opinion – female as well as male. In the end, it took World War I (1914–18) to change attitudes and get the first British women the vote in 1918.

"Freedom is learnt by practising it."

Clara Campoamor, Spanish suffrage campaigner (1888–1972)

NEW ZEALAND
1893
AUSTRALIA
1902
FINLAND
1906

UK
1918 (PROPERTY-
OWNING WOMEN
OVER 30)

1928 (ALL
WOMEN OVER 21)

THE MARCH TO FEMINISM

WOMEN AROUND THE WORLD GOT

Changing attitudes

New Zealand was the first country to grant some women suffrage, in 1893, thanks in part to prominent social activist Kate Sheppard. Nine years later Australia did the same. More countries followed suit after the end of World War I, with a wave of new suffrage laws being passed in the 1920s and 1930s. In Spain, women won the vote in 1931, but lost many legal rights during the fascist dictatorship (1939–75). Women in southern Europe and large parts of Asia and South America had to wait until after World War II and into the 1950s before the vote reached them.

INDIA
1950

GHANA
1954

SAUDI
ARABIA
2011

US
1920

SPAIN
1931

BRAZIL
1934

FRANCE
1944
ITALY
1945

COURAGE
CALLS TO
COURAGE
EVERYWHERE

THE VOTE AT VERY DIFFERENT TIMES

See also: 18–19, 20–21, 24–25, 28–29, 140–141

Slow progress

Even in countries that had allowed some women the vote, exclusions still applied. In Australia, Aboriginal women were unable to share the rights of white women until 1962, and it took decades before African American and Native American women could vote in all US states. Many African countries were only able to grant all women the vote once they had gained independence from colonial rule. In other parts of the world, harsh regimes severely restricted both female and male suffrage until the late 20th century. By 1980, most countries allowed women to vote, but in some places it is still difficult for women to safely exercise this right.

Emmeline Pankhurst

1858–1928

After more than 20 years campaigning peacefully with the British women's movement to get suffrage (the right to vote) for women, Emmeline Pankhurst decided that bold action was the only way to achieve their goal. "Deeds, not words" became the motto of the group she formed – the suffragettes.

> "We are here, not because we are law-breakers; we are here in our efforts to become law-makers."

Radical breakaway

Groups working to get the vote for women in the UK had been active since the 1860s, but had seen little progress. Peaceful marches no longer made the headlines. In 1903, Emmeline Pankhurst and her daughters, Christabel, Sylvia, and Adela, started the Women's Social and Political Union (WSPU), nicknamed the suffragettes.

Revolutionary tactics

Having grown up in a middle-class family interested in politics, Pankhurst socialized with intellectuals and activists, even Russian revolutionaries. Inspired by their militant tactics, Pankhurst encouraged the WSPU women to protest in ways that couldn't be ignored, from chaining themselves to fences to setting fire to letter boxes and homes of politicians. They were often arrested but continued their protest in prison by going on hunger strikes, refusing to eat. Guards would force-feed the women by holding them down and pushing a feeding tube through their nose – a form of torture.

Turning point

In 1914, at the start of World War I, Pankhurst halted violent protests and worked with the government to recruit women into the war effort. In 1918, property-owning women over 30 got the vote, extended to all women over 21 in 1928 – two weeks after Pankhurst's death from poor health due to years of fierce campaigning.

Mother and daughter
Emmeline and Christabel Pankhurst are seen here during one of their many stays in prison. To avoid creating martyrs, the government released women weak from a hunger strike, only to re-arrest them as soon as they got better.

Making noise
Emmeline Pankhurst is arrested while trying to hand in a petition to the king, 21 May 1914. The physical violence that the suffragettes encountered, and were prepared to endure, kept their cause in the spotlight.

WOMEN at war

The two world wars that shook the 20th century were on a scale never seen before. As more and more men were sent to the front to fight, thousands of women were recruited to take up jobs they left behind in factories and farms, and to support the war effort on the home front – giving them the opportunity to prove themselves in the world of work.

Doing their bit

Working-class women had always worked, particularly in textile factories and domestic service, but in World War I (1914–18) many more women entered the workforce to help with the manpower crisis at home. They became nurses, teachers, and also took on jobs previously denied to them because of their sex – a huge number worked with dangerous explosives in munitions plants, others worked as bus drivers, on the railways, in heavy industry, as clerical workers and shop assistants, and on the land. New roles were opened up to women – in England, the first women police officers served during World War I. The women's work was crucial to the economic survival of their countries.

Women were proud to be playing an active part in the war effort, and demonstrating that they were capable of dangerous and difficult work. Jobs also took women out of the home and involved them in a broader world than they had known before. Some joined munitions factory sports teams, and ladies' football matches often drew big crowds.

"Land girls" helped to keep wartime food production going.

Clerical jobs offered new opportunities.

Heavy work in factories and shipyards was not just for men.

Work in munitions factories was part of women's war.

Women could be codebreakers – on lower pay than men.

DURING THE TWO WORLD WARS, WOMEN SPRANG INTO ACTION

But when the men came back at the end of the war, it was taken for granted that women would return to the largely domestic lives they had lived before, and many did. The opportunities that had opened up seemed to be fading away.

Fighting women

Twenty years later, World War II (1939–45) broke out, and women went back to work. The difference this time was that hundreds of thousands of women joined, or were conscripted into, the armed forces. In the UK and US, women in the forces did not see combat, but worked in auxilliary roles as searchlight operators, in anti-aircraft units, and as interpreters of aerial photographs.

In Russia women did see combat, including 2,000 female snipers who were sent to the front, and several female air force units. In Nazi-occupied France, Italy, and Poland many women took part in the Resistance Movement, facing daily danger.

It took two terrible world wars to give some women their first taste of the opportunity that work can bring. Although in the immediate post-war years, women's employment returned to almost pre-war levels, the point had been made: women could hold their own on the job.

NIGHT WITCHES

In 1941, Soviet navigator Marina Rashkova founded an all-female regiment of bomber pilots, whose stealth operations earned them the nickname "night witches". By the end of the war, many of the pilots had flown more than 800 missions and were regarded as national heroes.

In World War II, women pilots ferried warplanes to and from airbases.

See also: 22–25, 100–103

Some of the first protests for equal pay and rights took place during World War I.

Female ambulance drivers braved the worst danger zones.

Nurses went to the front lines to care for wounded troops.

AND CHANGED LONG-HELD PREJUDICES ABOUT GENDER AND WORK

(Un)Equal RIGHTS!

In the mid-19th century feminists began to fight for a fairer society in which women had the same legal rights as men. Up until then women had few rights. They were not allowed to vote, and in some societies they were considered to be the property of their fathers or husbands.

Who holds the power?

The call for equality came because for centuries men had more rights than women. They could own property, and many had access to an education and were allowed to vote. The message was that women were somehow lesser beings than men, and if a group is viewed as unequal, it makes it easier to justify treating them unfairly. For decades feminists fought for women's equality socially, politically, and economically. They contested the idea that biological differences between men and women justified their unequal treatment. Feminists argue that the inequality women have experienced is in fact due to social structures and institutions that oppress women and preserve patriarchal power.

THE FAMOUS FIVE

Although most Canadian women had the right to vote by the 1920s, they were far from gaining political equality. Then, in 1929, five women in Alberta were responsible for a change in the law that finally gave women legal status as "persons". The law previously referred to a "person" as "he", which meant that women weren't legally recognized.

A modest proposal

A key area of the struggle for women's equality was, and is, the law. The law shapes our social, political, economic, and cultural lives. Although it is commonly believed that legal changes bring about changes in attitudes, this is not always the case. American suffragette Alice Paul wrote the Equal Rights Amendment (ERA) in 1923. It proposed changes to the US constitution that would invalidate many laws that discriminated against women. Paul introduced the ERA to Congress because she was frustrated that although women had been given the vote three years earlier, discrimination was still happening. With the help of American feminist Betty Friedan and politician Shirley Chisholm, who were strong supporters of the ERA and helped to turn the tide in its favour, the ERA was passed by Congress in 1972, nearly 50 years later. This was a significant victory, however, when the deadline came for ratification in 1982, only 35 of the necessary 38 states supported it, so the ERA failed. In fact, the proposed changes to the constitution still haven't taken effect, and today, feminists continue to fight for it.

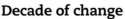

> ## "Human rights are women's rights, and women's rights are human rights."
>
> ### Hillary Clinton, US politician (1995)

THE LAW SHOULD ENFORCE GENDER EQUALITY BUT THE SCALES ARE NOT YET BALANCED

Decade of change

The 1970s were particularly exciting in terms of changes to the law as feminists highlighted inequalities in such things as pay and the right to divorce, and pushed for something to be done about them. A key moment was the 1975 UN World Conference on Women, which highlighted the discrimination women experienced worldwide. Four years later, the UN General Assembly adopted the Convention on the Elimination of All Forms of Discrimination Against Women. This international treaty requires the nations agreeing to its terms to take measures to end discrimination against women in all forms, including enforcing laws to protect them against violence and increasing women's political participation.

In name only

While these have been positive steps, feminists argue that changes to law and legislation have not been sufficient to achieve gender equality. Firstly, because passing a law and getting it enforced are two separate things. For example, the gender pay gap still exists in nations where discrimination in pay has been illegal for 40 years. Secondly, feminists argue that because the law is mostly controlled and written by men, it reflects male bias and does not further the interests of women. British Sociologist Carol Smart argues that the wording of laws does not always adequately protect women – perhaps one reason why rape in marriage has only recently been recognized as a crime in some countries. According to Smart, legal definitions of rape are too narrow, they do not accurately reflect women's experience of assault, and it is usually the victim who has to prove that she didn't give consent. So while we are told that women have achieved legal equality in some countries, arguably there's a long way to go.

See also: 22–23, 108–109, 114–115

Women's
LIBERATION

In the decades after World War II, amid global political reorganization, women united to build on the demands of earlier 20th-century feminists. Influenced by the civil rights movement and student protests, women of the 1960s campaigned for equality and social justice with renewed vigour.

See also: 22–23, 66–67, 84–85, 106–107

The personal is political

In what became known as the "second-wave" feminism of the 1960s and 1970s, feminist campaigners achieved their highest profile since the days of the suffragettes. Soon referred to as the Women's Liberation Movement (or Women's Lib) the activists of this era took the slogan "the personal is political" as their starting point. Influenced by thinkers such as French philosopher Simone de Beauvoir and American writer Betty Friedan, they held that many aspects of a woman's personal life, including family, sexuality, and work, were controlled by sexist power politics. Other major influences included theorists such as American activist Kate Millett, who wrote about how women internalize their own oppression.

Consciousness raising

"False consciousness" was an important concept for activists. This is a mindset that leaves women unable to see unjust social systems, such as racism and male dominance, for what they really are, and so they do not question them. For second-wave feminists, consciousness-raising (CR) groups were a significant part of their agenda, making women aware of the unfairnesses that they faced every day. In CR groups, women met to share and compare personal stories of childbirth, motherhood, male attitudes, and relationships, often finding they had common

experiences of isolation, shame, or fear of violence. As the groups developed, they went on to discuss and analyse how ideas on gender were largely created by society. They also established support groups for women in difficult or threatening circumstances.

SECOND-WAVE FEMINISM ENCOURAGED

Second-wave achievements

The Women's Liberation Movement added its collective voice to many of the social campaigns of the time. For example, feminists were strongly supportive of the civil rights movement for racial equality, backed anti-war protests, and fought for amendments to laws that would give women equal rights in areas such as employment and pay. They helped to raise awareness of marginalized issues such as domestic violence and sexual harassment, and had a significant role in the liberalization of divorce laws. Second-wave feminism also led to increasing numbers of women in educational roles and the introduction of women's studies as an academic subject.

Sexual liberation?

Among the social changes that second-wave feminists demanded and helped to initiate, perhaps most important to women were those that gave them more control over their own bodies. In many countries, feminist campaigning helped women gain access to

> # "Let us begin the revolution and let us begin it with love."
>
> **Kate Millett , *Sexual Politics* (1970)**

safe, legal abortions, reducing the fear of unwanted pregnancy and the dangers of "backstreet" operations. The introduction of the contraceptive pill made further personal choices available to women about when, or if, to have children, although when first introduced the pill was prescribed mainly to married women.

These measures – much talked about as the "sexual revolution" of the 1960s – may have brought heterosexual women new freedoms, but were often defined in sexist ways. For example, women were expected to be less cautious about having sexual relationships and to be in charge of contraception, which took the pressure off men to share responsibility.

WOMEN TO DISCUSS PERSONAL ISSUES

THE BRA-BURNING MYTH

The Women's Liberation Movement of the 1970s is associated with the image of feminists whipping off their bras and burning them as a gesture of freedom. But bra-burning was a media myth, probably initiated by an exaggerated report of a feminist protest at a beauty contest in the US, when women threw their bras and other female items in a bin.

Gloria Steinem

Born 1934

The figurehead for American feminism in the 1960s and 1970s, and co-founder of Ms. magazine, Gloria Steinem is one of the US's most famous feminists. Unlike many feminists at the time, who focused on the issues of white, middle-class women, Steinem believed that gender equality must include women of all classes and races. She remains a passionate activist, still speaking out against injustices in society.

> ## "Women aren't going to be equal outside the home until men are equal in it."

Early insight

Thanks to her father's urge to take his family on the road, Gloria grew up experiencing many different places, people, and situations. Economic hardship, her parents' divorce when she was 10, and her mother's struggle to support a family while coping with depression, are also likely to have influenced her views on the limited opportunities of most women. Her father's unconventional attitude towards social norms might also have inspired her to question established ideas on women's role and status.

Print the word

Her career as a journalist gave Gloria Steinem a platform for speaking out on women's equality. She expressed her ideas in an article published in *New York* magazine in 1969, which urged readers to put equality for women at the top of the political agenda. In *Ms.* magazine, she wrote and published influential articles on women's rights. Steinem also wrote about "hidden", rarely discussed subjects such as menstruation, FGM, abortion, child abuse, and violence against women.

Political campaigns

Steinem has also been involved in other political causes. She joined protests to end the Vietnam War and South African apartheid. She has promoted LGBTQ rights and pushed for sex education in US schools. Steinem is still fighting for feminism today, and took part in the Women's March on Washington, DC, in 2017.

Equal power

In 1972, Gloria Steinem co-founded the legendary feminist magazine *Ms.* with African American activist Dorothy Pitman Hughes. The pair spoke together at events throughout the 1970s to promote equal rights.

Activist stance

In her early career as a journalist, Steinem wrote on a range of subjects, including an article on pop culture in 1965, for which this photo was taken. Soon, however, she came to concentrate on feminist issues.

Living
WITHOUT MEN

In the 1970s, second-wave feminists started calling into question the relationships between women and men. If our society is patriarchal (based on men having all the power) and women are oppressed by male-dominated institutions, including traditional family structures, is it possible for women to have relationships with men that are equal?

 See also: 14–15, 66–67, 70–71

The sexual is political

In 1970, Australian feminist Germaine Greer sent shock waves through society by challenging male domination in the Western nuclear family. In her book *The Female Eunuch* Greer argued that women should reject the roles expected of them as wives and mothers and take control of their own lives. This led other feminists to question the nature of their relationships with men, too. In the same year, in her book *Sexual Politics* Kate Millett suggested that all relationships between men and women were based on power – that society works on stereotypes of the submissive female and dominant male and this is the basis for key social institutions such as marriage, religion, and education. Millett points out that motherhood, childcare, and the right to contraception, among other issues, are central to maintaining women's oppression. However this political issue is hidden because patriarchal, or male-dominated, institutions, such as the government and the media, present this relationship between men and women as "natural".

> ## "Status ought not to be measured by a woman's ability to attract and snare a man."
>
> **Germaine Greer, *The Female Eunuch* (1970)**

Compulsory heterosexuality?

For some, one way to avoid participating in this gender inequality was to reject heterosexuality itself – what American feminist Marilyn Frye called "separatism". In 1979, the British Leeds Revolutionary Feminist Group coined the term "political lesbianism". Their argument was that women should remove themselves from social and sexual connections with men, without necessarily having sexual relationships with women.

These ideas were set out by American feminist poet Adrienne Rich in her essay "Compulsory Heterosexuality and Lesbian Existence" (1980). Rich suggests that heterosexuality is not necessarily the

line, to women who have sexual as well as political relationships with women at the other end. In other words, Rich believes that every woman has a lesbian potential.

Lesbian feminism, however, was not always widely accepted. In 1969, American feminist Betty Friedan argued that lesbians constituted a "lavender menace" that threatened the respectability of feminism. Other feminists criticized Rich for idealizing lesbianism and ignoring the oppressions that lesbians experienced. Some lesbians were also outraged by Rich's suggestion that lesbianism could be any woman's choice, or that it could be defined as simply not having sex with men.

POLITICAL LESBIANS SUGGEST THAT ALL WOMEN HAVE A LESBIAN POTENTIAL

natural choice for women, but rather it is imposed on them. Society convinces women that marriage is inevitable, helped by the "ideology of heterosexual romance" – stories that end with a "happily ever after" for heterosexual couples, for example in fairy tales, Hollywood films, and pop songs. In these stories women are also taught that friendships and bonds between women are not as important as romantic love between men and women, and that lesbianism is deviant – instead, women are encouraged to see other women as rivals for men's affections.

Lesbian continuum

To counter this, Rich proposed a "lesbian continuum" – a line upon which women can place themselves, from political lesbians (those who identify as heterosexual but reject men on political grounds) at one end of the

ABOLISHING GENDER

In the 1980s, French feminist lesbian theorist Monique Wittig argued that in order for women to be truly independent from men, the categories of "man" and "woman" must be rejected. In her view, ideas about sexual difference are used to hold up heterosexual relationships as the norm – relationships that according to Wittig subjugate women.

BACKLASH!

Throughout history, periods of progress have typically been followed by anti-feminist backlash. In the 1980s, old ideas about masculinity and traditional family roles resurfaced with a vengeance in the media, pushing back against the gains women had made.

War against women

American journalist Susan Faludi, in her 1991 book *Backlash: The Undeclared War Against American Women*, analysed the ways popular culture of the 1980s presented feminism and its impacts. She argued that the overriding message from the media and popular culture was that feminism had failed women: greater independence had come at the price of loneliness, childlessness, and confusion about their place in the world. Print publications carried articles that blamed feminism for women's every woe. Hollywood films portrayed independent women as dangerous and unstable. And self-help books stated that women were unfulfilled because they were no longer performing their "natural" role. The overall message was that feminism threatened family life and was making women stressed and unhappy.

Post-feminist world

At the time, politics in the West was dominated by an ideology called neoliberalism, exemplified by British Prime Minister Margaret Thatcher and US President Ronald Reagan. Neoliberalism prized individualism and personal choice, but also viewed individuals as responsible for what they made of their lives. By implication, gender was no obstacle to getting ahead. The previous decade had seen many legal changes around

FASHION COMPLEX

British sociologist Angela McRobbie has talked about a "complexification of backlash" from the mid-1990s. In her view, the "fashion and beauty complex" controls young women. They appear to have gained equality, but consumer culture's obsession with femininity encourages them to focus on the self, not the common good.

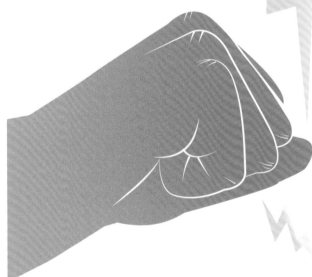

THROUGH HISTORY, PERIODS OF PROGRESS

> ## "How did feminism become a national 'dirty word'?"
>
> Debra Baker Beck, *The F Word* (1998)

birth control, pay, and divorce, which benefitted women. This progress in social policy, combined with the new politics of choice, led some to argue that feminism had done its work, but that equality was making women unhappy. Feminists refer to this as post-feminism. Post-feminism and neoliberalism see competition as natural. Women are viewed as being in competition, making feminist solidarity impossible.

Job done?

In fact, Faludi pointed out American women were still not equal at all. In the workplace, they were still paid less than men, with the majority working in traditional "female" roles. Access to contraception had declined. Education funding, such as college grants, still favoured men. In many US states, it was still legal for a man to rape his wife. In her view, the anti-feminist backlash was occurring not because women had achieved equal rights but precisely because of the increased possibility that they might. The messages in the media about how feminism was making women unhappy were a form of "pre-emptive strike" to prevent women from achieving true equality.

Media manipulation

Many feminists have examined the idea of ongoing anti-feminist backlash. American academic Debra Baker Beck argued in 1998 that negative depictions in the mass media of assertive women and stereotyped portrayals of feminists as angry man-haters accounted for people's reluctance to identify as feminist. British sociologist Angela McRobbie (see box) has observed that feminism was mocked and despised during the 1990s, so that girls did not want to identify with it. Even today, few women described themselves as feminist – only 9 per cent of British women, according to a 2016 survey by UK campaign group the Fawcett Society. Could it be that the negative messages are hitting their mark?

See also: 118–119, 128–129 →

HAVE BEEN FOLLOWED BY BACKLASH

Girl POWER!

In 1996, "girl power" was the phrase on everyone's lips. Born out of an underground punk movement, this new brand of feminism soon spread its roots through popular culture. It aimed to show women they could be fun, independent, and in control of their own lives. But was this girl power message truly empowering women?

Angry grrrls

A few years before the rise of "girl power", an underground scene of artists and punk musicians emerged in the US. One prominent group was the Guerrilla Girls – a collective of feminist art activists formed in 1985. Appearing in public wearing gorilla masks for anonymity, they designed striking posters that exposed sexual and racial inequalities in the art world – for example, in 1986 they noted that only four commercial galleries in New York showed work by black women.

In the early 1990s, another influential movement rose out of the US Pacific Northwest punk music scene. Known as Riot Grrrl, it published its own feminist manifesto and fanzines that addressed key women's issues, such as eating disorders, relationships, and sexual abuse. Other comic books and zines by women, such as *Girl Power* and *Girl Germs* became popular emblems of this "angry girl" movement. Bands such as Bikini Kill further promoted the cause, but the mainstream media turned against them due to their shock tactics, such as scrawling "slut" across their bodies.

See also: 30–31

Punk feminism

"Revolution grrrl style now" – Bikini Kill

"Female by birth. Feminist by choice" – Guerrilla Girls

GRRRLS!

WOMEN EXPRESSED FEMINIST VIEWS

The Spice Girls' debut hit "Wannabe" is still the best-selling single by a female group.

GIRL POWER!

IN PERFORMANCE AND POSTER ART

LADIES FIRST

Rap music in the 1980s was male-dominated and sexist. In 1988, MC Lyte (right) became the first female solo rapper to release an album, while rap artist Queen Latifah used songs such as "Ladies First" (1989) to challenge sexism.

Variety is the spice of life

Enter five women from the UK: the Spice Girls. Their light-hearted songs focused around female friendship may not have addressed the serious issues that other female bands had, but they resonated with audiences. The band were also one of only a few all-female groups to break into a music scene that had so far been largely populated by boy bands. As "Spice mania" took over, the activism of Riot Grrrl morphed into a more popular, upbeat idea of empowerment that focused less on the downsides of being a woman.

Feminism recast

Some feminists criticized the Spice Girls for reinforcing sexist ideas of what women should look like, and pointed out that their lyrics were written for them (by men). The band was part of a larger shift in the feminist movement – an aspect of third-wave feminism that was termed "lipstick feminism" by its critics. Characterized by "sheroes" such as Buffy the Vampire Slayer, this new feminism attempted to redefine women as both girly and powerful. It was a popular message, but seen by many as too linked to consumerism – urging girls to buy products to "empower" them.

Today, there are many feminist performers in the public eye, such as Beyoncé. But punk subculture's influence has also spread, as seen in the actions of Russian feminist punk band Pussy Riot who, in 2012, challenged their nation's sexism and homophobia in their expletive-filled songs.

Everyday SEXISM

Sexism describes prejudice based on sex, most commonly against women and girls. Sexist behaviours and attitudes reinforce stereotypical gender roles. Everyday sexism can range from discriminating against someone due to their sex, to sexual harassment in the street or workplace.

Sexist culture

Many women and girls minimize their own experience of sexism, often because they do not recognize certain behaviours as sexist. In 2012, British activist Laura Bates set up the Everyday Sexism Project in order to change this. It began with a website where women and girls could share their experiences, and it soon became clear that sexist behaviour is worryingly common. It happens on the street, in schools, colleges, at work, in politics, and online. Sexism may be intentional or unintentional, but behaviour such as ignoring women in meetings, using the pronoun "he" when discussing professionals, passing women over for promotion or making them conform to sexist dress codes all serve to support and normalize a sexist culture. The project now operates in more than 25 countries.

Whose streets?

Many of the Everyday Sexism contributors described their experiences of street harassment – being subject to unwanted comments or gestures from strangers in public. Australian academic Raewyn Connell sees this type of behaviour as reinforcing the idea that public spaces are male spaces, where women are made to feel unwelcome unless they comply. Women are cast as commodities for the entertainment and pleasure of men and are expected to play along – told to "cheer up"

HEY, SEXY!

In 1981, sexual harassment at work was established as a violation of US civil rights.

GIRLS ARE SUBJECTED TO A STEADY DRIP-DRIP-DRIP OF SEXISM

> ## "The background noise of harassment... connects to violence and rape."
>
> Laura Bates, *Everyday Sexism* (2014)

and branded uptight or humourless if they complain. But while it is often dismissed as trivial, many feminists believe that street harassment must be understood as male control of female bodies, playing a role in creating a society that tolerates and normalizes sexual assault and abuse.

Longstanding sexism

The findings of Bates' project were not new. In 1989, British human rights activist and writer Joan Smith's collection of essays *Misogynies* charted the many ways women faced sexism – for example, films that glamorized violence against women, and images of topless women in the media. Almost 30 years later, Bates' work revealed that little had changed. Conviction rates for the few rape cases that are reported are still low, TV still revels in violence against women, and advertisements and magazines still portray women in sexual images. In fact, Smith thinks that woman-hating is now more seething and widespread than ever before.

Enough is enough

When women become aware of the sexism that they experience, they can stop accepting it as "normal". Social media platforms such as Twitter provide a place where women can tell their stories and people can listen on an unprecedented scale. With an ongoing dialogue about everyday sexism, attitudes and behaviours may start to change.

SEXISM IN SCHOOLS

The Everyday Sexism Project found that girls in schools find it very hard to stand up to sexual harassment. Laura Bates observes that this is because of the sheer strength of gender stereotypes. When boys make unwelcome, often sexual, comments on how girls look, girls may normalize it as "boys being boys".

See also: 42–43, 92–93

#METoo

The #MeToo movement against sexual harassment and assault kicked off in October 2017, when women involved in Hollywood and the media began to share stories about the abuse they had experienced at the hands of powerful men. The movement rapidly spread and became a powerful tool in demonstrating how widespread sexual harassment is.

Solidarity in sharing

African American activist Tarana Burke first started using the phrase "Me Too" in 2006, as part of a campaign to empower young women of colour who had experienced sexual abuse. Fast-forward to Hollywood in 2017, where film producer Harvey Weinstein faced allegations about misconduct towards women he had worked with. These included accusations of sexual assault and rape, for which he went on trial in May 2018. He denies all allegations. As part of a campaign to raise awareness of sexism and misogyny in the media, the actress Alyssa Milano, who wasn't aware of the phrase's origins, asked women to use the Twitter hashtag #MeToo to share their experiences and show just how common abuse was. It quickly became clear that many other men were accused of abusing their positions of power. #MeToo soon became a global phenomenon.

Witch hunt?

The #MeToo campaign has faced some criticism. Many prominent men, including US President Donald Trump (himself accused of misconduct), have claimed it has gone too far. In an open letter

BREAK THE SILENCE TOGETHER

> ## "Every single instance of sexual harassment needs to be dealt with."
>
> Tarana Burke, founder of Me Too (2018)

TIME'S UP

In the wake of #MeToo, the Time's Up organization was set up to campaign against harassment and for equality in the workplace. Celebrities wore black to red carpet events to show their support. At the 2018 Cannes Film Festival actor Cate Blanchett led the Time's Up protest.

to newspaper *Le Monde*, actress Catherine Deneuve and 99 other French women argued that men should be "free to hit on" women. They accused #MeToo and its French equivalent #BalanceTonPorc (Call Out Your Pig) of being puritanical and said the male sexual urge is "wild and aggressive". Controversial Australian feminist Germaine Greer claimed that the instances of harassment reported were minor, calling on women to stop whinging and toughen up.

Other critics have argued that #MeToo is for privileged white women and ignores the abuse of marginalized women, or that it confuses harassment and rape. However, as feminist activist and author of *Surviving Sexual Violence* (1988) Liz Kelly suggests, all sexual violence can be seen as part of a continuum – one form can lead to another.

> By the end of 2017, 1.7 million tweets including the hashtag #MeToo had been sent.

Stronger together

The #MeToo movement has shown women that solidarity is powerful and can bring about social change. Millions of women who have found the courage to talk about their painful experiences have felt empowered by simply speaking out. These women recognize that they have all been harmed by the same forces of sexism, and together demand that these forces be defeated. When so many women have experienced the same kind of sexist behaviour from men, it becomes easier to believe that the problem goes beyond individuals, and instead relates to a sexist culture. Publicly recognizing the problem may help to stop sexual harassment being seen as normal and put an end to it.

See also: 40–41, 88–89

SHARING IS EMPOWERING

WOMEN SPEAK UP IN UNISON

Chimamanda Ngozi Adichie

Born 1977

Chimamanda Ngozi Adichie writes and speaks about her experiences as a black female and what it means to live as a woman in the 21st century. The Nigerian-born author has written several bestselling books, and has become a spokesperson for feminism through her social media presence.

> **"I have chosen to no longer be apologetic... I want to be respected in all of my femaleness because I deserve to be."**

An African in America

Adichie was born in Nigeria and moved to the US to study at age 19. She wrote her first novel *Purple Hibiscus* (2004) at 26, followed by her award-winning novel *Half of a Yellow Sun* (2006). Adichie's books are studied in US schools and she has also become a media spokesperson on racism and sexism.

We should all be feminists

In 2012, Adichie caused a sensation with her TED Talk (online talks about "ideas worth spreading") "We Should All be Feminists", in which she urged everyone to act against sexism. She said "A feminist is a man or a woman who says, yes, there's a problem with gender as it is today and we must fix it... All of us, women and men, must do better." Her message spread around the world on social media, attracting around four million views. Pop star Beyoncé sampled her speech, fashion label Dior used it as a slogan on T-shirts, and in Sweden it was made into a book and a copy was given to every 16-year-old.

Being yourself

One of Adichie's strongest messages is that women and men both suffer as a result of the gender roles we adhere to. She says we teach men to be afraid of fear and weakness, and we teach girls "to shrink themselves", to have ambition but not too much, so they don't threaten men. Adichie argues that in order for men and women to be their true selves, we must all be committed to unlearning gender roles.

Award-winning author
Adichie was first confronted with racism when she moved to the US in 1996. She wrote about her experiences in her award-winning book *Americanah* (2013).

International role model
Adichie, seen here at the Eighth Annual Women In The World Summit in New York, US, in 2017, is a powerful female role model. Her personal stories illuminate some of the most pressing international issues faced by women today.

BODY and IDENTITY

Are WOMEN and MEN the same?

All in the MIND?

Are GIRLS BORN or MADE?

Is GENDER fixed?

What does it mean to be a woman? Feminism has questioned whether gender identity is a result of nature or nurture. Many feminists believe much of what is assumed to be natural female behaviour is created by society's expectations of women. Others have looked at how gender intersects with other aspects of identity and asked how we can make feminism inclusive to all women.

INTERSECTING identities

WOMANISM

Are **WOMEN** and **MEN** the same?

What makes a woman or a man? The quick answer for many is biology, but is that a useful explanation? How different are we, and what impact do physical differences have on our expectations for men and women?

Body matters

On average, men are taller, heavier, and hairier than women, and there are obvious reproductive differences – men have testes and a penis; women have ovaries, a vagina, breasts, and broader hips. People often think of male bodies and female bodies as fitting neatly into two distinct categories, but in reality there is plenty of overlap: some women grow facial hair, for example, while some men may have a large amount of breast tissue. On top of that, cultural norms emphasize the difference between men and women, for example through social pressure on women to remove their natural body hair.

It's different for girls

A key difference between male and female bodies is their roles in reproduction. For most girls, puberty means the beginning of menstruation in preparation for possible pregnancy and childbirth. Radical second-wave feminists saw childbirth as a source of women's oppression. In *The Dialectic of Sex* (1970), Canadian American feminist Shulamith Firestone suggested that women's biological features had put them in a class below men because women became dependent on men for support during pregnancy, childbirth, and childrearing. Firestone argued that technology, such

See also: 50–51, 52–53, 78–79, 102–103

SOCIETY ENCOURAGES MEN TO BE STRONG

as birth control and artificial reproduction, could liberate women so that "genital differences between human beings would no longer matter culturally".

It is not only childbearing that has been used to restrict women – taboos around menstruation in many cultures restricts women's movements even today. Many major religions insist women should not attend a temple if on their period, and some forbid women from entering the kitchen, touching or sleeping near other people, or attending school at these times.

Biological essentialism

Some people believe that other perceived differences between the sexes – attributes often associated with each sex such as assertiveness and leadership in men and empathy in women – are the result of differences in female and male biology. This is known as "biological

STRONG LIKE A GIRL

American feminist Iris Marion Young argued that even if there is physical variation between men and women, it may be exaggerated by years of using our bodies differently. Girls are taught that they are fragile and vulnerable, so they are often more cautious in their movements, and thus never exploit their physical potential.

essentialism". There is no scientific evidence for these perceived differences. Feminists vigorously contest biological essentialism because it paints "masculine" and "feminine" traits as innate, and has been used to justify women's subordinate position in society. Instead, many take a "constructivist" approach: they view gender differences as a product of society (see pp 52–53).

No limits

While physical variation exists between different men and women, rather than highlighting the limits of women's and men's bodies, we should focus on what they are capable of and judge them on their individual merits. To make assumptions about someone because of their sex fails to make the most of and reward the skills of each individual.

WOMEN ARE ENCOURAGED TO BE NURTURING

> ## "Women's bodily differences from men have... served as excuses for structural inequalities."
>
> **Iris Marion Young, *On Female Body Experience: "Throwing Like a Girl" and Other Essays* (2005)**

All in the MIND?

To many people, men and women seem so different that they may as well be different species. The idea that men and women think and feel differently is deeply entrenched in our society. But is there really such a thing as a male brain and a female brain?

Gendered brain?

There are some physical differences between men's and women's brains. On average, men's brains are larger and heavier than women's (in keeping with the fact that men's bodies overall are on average larger than women's). The size of specific areas of the brain vary between men and women, too. The cerebral cortex (responsible for things like language and intelligence) is typically thicker in women, and the hippocampus (responsible for memory formation) is larger in men. However, scientists don't know whether or how these differences affect the way men and women behave.

Hot topic

Some academics, such as British psychologist Simon Baron-Cohen, have suggested that variations in male and female brains produce different traits in men and women – for example, inclining men to be more competitive and women to be more nurturing. Others have claimed that the fact that men seem to have better spacial awareness and numeracy skills, while woman are better at

communication or empathy, shows their brains function differently. However, these suggestions are controversial. While men and women do perform differently at certain cognitive tasks, there is no evidence that this is due to innate differences in the brain. The idea that there is such a thing as a typical male or female brain is sometimes referred to as neurosexism.

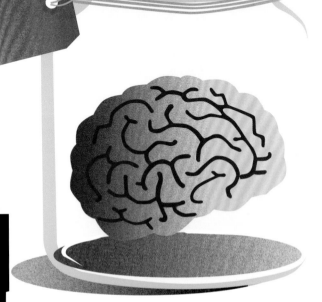

> ## "The brain is a unisex organ."
>
> Lise Eliot (2018)

THERE IS NO SUCH THING AS A

Thinking outside the box

In 2015, Israeli psychologist Daphna Joel carried out a study that showed there were more similarities than differences between male and female brains. Using brain scans of 1,400 people, researchers looked for variations between the brains of men and women. They found 29 regions that seemed different and coded them either "male" or "female". However, most brains displayed a unique combination of both types of characteristic and could not obviously be identified as belonging to a particular gender. Joel concluded that human brains cannot be categorized into two distinct types. Most individual brains are just that – individual.

Neuroplasticity

Trying to draw links between differences in brain structure and behaviour is further complicated by the fact that a person's brain changes over the course of their lifetime, according to their experiences.

TESTOSTERONE REX

Higher levels of the hormone testosterone in men are said to make men more competitive, aggressive, and prone to risk-taking. In her book *Testosterone Rex* (2017), British psychologist Cordelia Fine argues that this is a myth. She argues that hormones are just one factor influencing behaviour and such "masculine" characteristics are not innate but socially constructed.

This idea that the brain changes depending on how you use it is known as neuroplasticity. Lise Eliot, an American professor of neuroscience, explores this idea in her book *Pink Brain, Blue Brain* (2009). She suggests that small differences in the brains of girls and boys at birth are amplified by the overwhelming onslaught of cultural expectations to behave in a certain way. Boys who are encouraged to play with puzzles and construction toys may develop better spatial awareness than girls who are given dolls and encouraged to be nurturing.

The dangers of myths

Ultimately, we do not know whether the slight differences between men's and women's brains have a bearing on their behaviour. Feminists have long argued that the traits we associate with men, such as aggression, or women, such as empathy, are not inherently masculine or feminine but the result of living in a society that rewards some characteristics in men and punishes them in women.

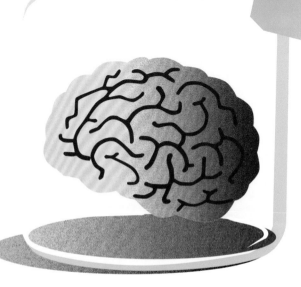

"MALE" OR "FEMALE" BRAIN

See also: 52–53, 78–79

Are GIRLS BORN or MADE?

Much of what causes us to view someone as male or female isn't about their sex at all, but their gender – the way they present themselves. When Simone de Beauvoir stated in 1949 that "one is not born, but rather becomes, a woman" she was paving the way for feminist theorists who examined whether gender was something innate or learned.

Sex, gender, and society

In *The Second Sex*, French feminist Simone de Beauvoir argued that society is constructed by men, so that we come to understand the concept of "woman" through male eyes. In such a world, the masculine is the privileged norm and the feminine becomes marginalized, or "other". De Beauvoir was talking about our concepts of men and women, not just as their physical bodies but everything that causes them to be perceived as masculine or feminine. She was saying that ideas about what makes a man or a woman come from society.

Sex and gender

Early second-wave feminists explored this idea of a person's gender as separate from their sex. Sex referred to biologically different categories of "male" and "female", based on chromosomes, hormones, and sex organs. Gender described a person's "masculinity" or "femininity", based on social and cultural differences – their behaviour, mannerisms, and presentation. Increasingly, gender was understood as separate from physical sex – something learned and influenced by society rather than innate. This idea is known as the "social construction" of gender. British sociologist Ann Oakley's *Sex, Gender and Society* (1972) suggested

See also: 48–49, 56–57, 72–73, 78–79

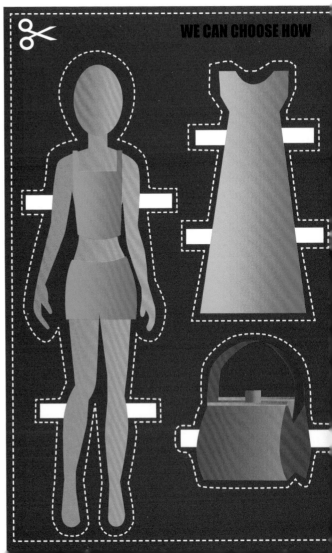

WE CAN CHOOSE HOW

that Western culture exaggerates gender differences and we should think of gender as being on a continuum rather than being two binary opposites.

Doing gender

Feminists showed the many ways in which gender is constructed through how we present ourselves – the clothes and hairstyles we wear; the hobbies and jobs we pick; and the names our parents give us. These things are culturally determined, not fixed. There's no reason that certain hairstyles should be for girls and others for boys, except that our culture says so. Feminists argue that these things suggest differences between the sexes. Judith Butler, an American gender theorist, sees gender as "performative". She suggests

BACHA POSH

In parts of Afghanistan, a country where boys are symbols of prestige with access to privileges such as education that are denied to girls, families may bring up a daughter as a son. Bacha posh, meaning "dressed like a boy", is a reaction to a gender-segregated society, but it shows how the trappings of gender are rooted in nurture rather than nature.

it is not based on any biological "essence" of being a man or woman but is something we construct in our social interactions, so it eventually comes to feel natural. In this sense, gender is something that we do, rather than something we are born with.

Beyond the gender binary

When we think about gender in this way it is possible to see that men and women can express both masculinity and femininity, so we can talk about female masculinity or male femininity. It is also possible to be female and not a woman (see pp 56–57). Furthermore, if gender is socially constructed, so are unequal power relations. If we can recognize this, it may be possible to transform society and move towards equality.

TO EXPRESS OUR GENDER

> **"We act and walk and speak and talk in ways that consolidate an impression of being a man or being a woman."**
>
> **Judith Butler (2011)**

Is GENDER fixed?

Feminists have long believed that gender stereotypes of how a man or a woman should be are harmful and restrictive. Now some also question the very idea that gender is just two fixed categories. Today, many feminists are working to make the ways we recognize gender more inclusive for everyone.

Born this way

One of the first questions people ask about a baby is whether it is a boy or a girl. But is gender really so simple? For a long time, theories assumed that gender was divided into two distinct categories of "masculine" and "feminine", related to two fixed categories for biological sex (male and female). However, people whose gender identity doesn't match the sex they were assigned at birth have existed throughout history and across many cultures. Today, they are referred to as transgender or trans. Those whose sex and gender identities do "match" are called cisgender.

Questioning gender ideas

Trans people may draw on various processes to affirm their gender identity, including hormone treatments and surgery, which can give them the opportunity to "transition" to the gender they identify with. However, for this to take place many countries require a diagnosis of "gender dysphoria" – a mental health condition defined as feeling one's gender is opposite to one's sex. While many trans people find these processes helpful, recent theory has emphasised that there is no right or wrong way to be trans. Many have championed new ways of thinking about gender, pointing out that some people identify as non-binary (not male or female) or gender fluid and use the pronouns "they/them". Trans activists have criticized the "medical model" of approaching gender, which sees being trans as a mental illness, and they have also criticized the cultural obsession with trans people's bodies.

US academic Sandy Stone has examined how transgender people are pressured to "pass" as cisgender by performing masculine or feminine gender stereotypes. She argues that the necessity of passing only exists because society is transphobic (prejudiced against trans people) and relies upon

See also: 52–53, 58–59, 72–73

CAITLYN JENNER

Perhaps the most famous US transgender woman, Caitlyn Jenner transitioned in 2015 and has done much work to raise awareness of the issues facing transgender people, arguing for a more inclusive society. The documentary *I Am Cait* followed Caitlyn's life after her transition.

categorizing everyone into only two opposing genders. For her, transgender identity can be a wholly unique gender identity that does not erase life before transition. Stone and other US theorists, such as Susan Stryker and Julia Serano, have also addressed transphobia within the women's movement. Some feminists see transgender women as "born male", and argue they have therefore benefitted from male privilege and do not share the same oppression as cisgender women. Stone says we need to be more inclusive and focus on the real issues, such as the need for legal and structural reform in how we classify gender and an awareness of the intersections between misogyny, transphobia, and other forms of oppression.

Transforming culture

Many issues still exist for trans people or those with other gender identities. For example, in the UK the Gender Recognition Act allows people to change their official gender, but only with a formal diagnosis of gender dysphoria.

> "There is no reason to assume that genders ought [...] to remain as two."
>
> Judith Butler, *Gender Trouble* (1990)

Activists have campaigned for self-identification measures that would allow people to do this without diagnosis, but have often been opposed. Transgender people (women of colour in particular) also experience high levels of abuse and violence. But many are working to improve the situation. The UK charity Mermaids provides support for families with trans children, and in recent years trans people have become much more visible in the media, generating new debates about gender.

GENDER CAN BE SEEN AS A SPECTRUM, RATHER THAN TWO FIXED CATEGORIES

INTERSECTING identities

Intersectionality is a word you may have seen and heard increasingly in the media. The term was first coined in 1989 by law professor Kimberlé Williams Crenshaw. She used the metaphor of the intersection, or crossroads, to explore how race and gender affect the lives of women in different ways. Today, disability, sexual orientation, class, and age are also included in this concept.

American origins

While women in general can be considered as an oppressed group, it is not as simple as that. Crenshaw, an American activist and legal scholar, argues that the experiences of black women are not the same as those of white women, and neither are they the same as those of black men. Black women are affected by both racism and sexism, not one or the other. She developed this theory after coming across a legal case in which an African American woman accused a company of not employing her because she was a black woman. The company argued that it wasn't racist – it had black employees; nor was it sexist – it had female employees. The case was thrown out. But the black workers were all men, and the female ones were all white. Crenshaw realized that since there was

> "There is no such thing as a single-issue struggle because we don't live single-issue lives."
>
> Audre Lorde (1982)

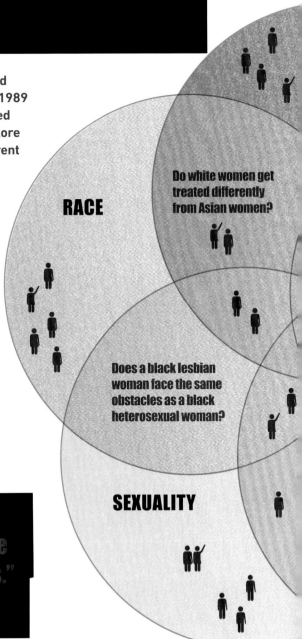

RACE

Do white women get treated differently from Asian women?

Does a black lesbian woman face the same obstacles as a black heterosexual woman?

SEXUALITY

HOW DO ASPECTS OF YOUR OWN IDENTITY AFFECT YOUR LIFE? AND WHAT ABOUT WOMEN AROUND YOU?

FEMINISM FOR ALL

American transgender actress and activist Laverne Cox speaks out on issues that affect transgender women in relation to feminism, intersectionality, and the #MeToo movement. Sharing her experiences of overcoming the obstacles facing transgender women of colour, she sends out positive messages on how to move forward.

GENDER

What is the job market like for a disabled transgender woman?

DISABILITY

Does an older disabled woman have to deal with the same prejudices as one who is younger?

AGE

no term for the double set of prejudices affecting this woman, the problem was hard to pinpoint and discuss. Crenshaw also looked at the issue of domestic violence to argue that feminist work has often overlooked black women's experiences and the black community has often ignored the gendered nature of the abuse.

Intersectionality in action

Since the term intersectionality was first used, the concept has been widened by academics, including Patricia Hill Collins, Sirma Bilge, and Rosemarie Garland-Thomson, to include ethnicity, class, poverty, sexuality, the whole gender spectrum, age, (dis)ability, and religion. We often think of these identities as straightforward binaries, or opposites – male/female, white/black, young/old, straight/gay, rich/poor. Within each set, one identity is considered the norm, and enjoys a privileged status in society, while the other may experience prejudice. Intersectional feminism considers how multiple identities may combine and interact to produce an individual's experience of discrimination. An older, white, middle-class, lesbian woman will face different prejudices to those experienced by a young, black, working-class, heterosexual woman. Intersectionality tries to take account of these overlapping identities so that no marginalized groups are overlooked.

See also: 42–43, 56–67, 62–63, 70–71, 88–89, 104–105

bell hooks

Born 1952

Growing up in a racially segregated community in the Southern US fuelled bell hooks' interest in the crossover between race, sex, and class that keeps black women oppressed. During her career as a scholar and author, she has written more than 30 books on racism, sexism, and feminism, including *Feminism is for Everybody*, which introduces the idea of feminism to a wide audience and is intended for men as well.

> **"Feminism is a movement to end sexism, sexist exploitation, and oppression."**

Challenging feminism

In 1981, hooks published *Ain't I a Woman?: Black women and feminism*. Its title was inspired by the famous speech, "'Ain't I a Woman", made by former slave Sojourner Truth (see p.20). Accusing the feminist movement of neglecting to involve black women, she also criticized the campaign for civil rights, saying that it kept black women in an inferior role.

Legacy

In 2014, hooks founded the bell hooks Institute for feminist studies at Berea College, Kentucky, US, where she is a professor. The Institute aims to celebrate her work and promote dialogue about feminist issues.

Black women in focus

Born Gloria Jean Watkins, bell hooks changed her name in honour of her maternal great-grandmother. She spells her name in lower-case letters to focus attention on her work rather than herself. As a child and teenager she experienced life in the US state of Kentucky at a time when civil rights for black people had yet to be made into law. She would soon come to the conclusion that black women were oppressed by both racism and sexism, and that this needed to change. For her, race and gender were inseparable.

Everybody's feminism

Although hooks is an academic, her style of writing is easy to read. Her aim is to explain complex subjects so that everyone can understand and get engaged. She is inclusive, too: in *Feminism is for Everybody* (2000), written as a handbook to counter the anti-feminist backlash, she explains how her feminism is not anti-male, just anti-sexism. She argues that feminism is a good thing for men, too, because it will free them from the pressure to conform to the stereotype of strong, masculine provider.

Trailblazer

An inspiring public speaker, bell hooks has influenced many other women through her work. She continues to speak out on topical issues, such as the representation of black women in the media.

WOMANISM

The feminist movement was and is a collective attempt to do something about male dominance, or oppression, but it has not been without its problems. Many have pointed out how the movement ignored the oppressions experienced by a range of women, and black women in particular. In response to this, womanism was born.

Whitewash?

There is no single cause of women's oppression and it affects women differently, depending on their identity. However, feminism in its various forms has not always adequately addressed the specific issues of race and class. The feminist movement has often focused on the lives of white, middle-class, heterosexual women. Coined by US novelist Alice Walker in 1983, the term "womanist" describes a kind of feminism that interprets the experiences of black women through their own eyes, based on their own values. Walker argued that non-black women, however well-meaning, cannot gain true insight of, or correctly describe, the particularities of the lives of African American (or any black) women; they lack the cultural understanding.

> ## "Womanist is to feminist as purple is to lavender."
>
> **Alice Walker, *In Search of Our Mother's Gardens* (1983)**

Bringing the house down

A few years before Walker gave the idea a name, Audre Lorde, a black, lesbian, feminist poet, had addressed an academic feminist conference with her speech "The Master's Tools will never Dismantle the Master's House", demanding that feminists take issues of racism, classism, and homophobia within the movement more seriously. She saw difference as both a challenge and a joy but asserted that from an African American experience, feminism was not as inclusive as it might have been, stating that "beyond sisterhood is still racism". She also pointed to how poverty kept many black women sidelined in the movement and how homophobia hurt both black and white women.

See also: 18–21, 60–61

WOMANISM REJOICES IN BLACK SISTERHOOD

Spelling it out

Lorde and Walker were talking about an intersectional approach. Kimberlé Crenshaw, who first used the term "intersectionality" (see p.58), said that feminist accounts of black women's experiences of domestic violence were not sufficient because they failed to look at intersections of gender and race. Intersectional thinking also means looking beyond the obvious, often violent, racism found in extreme right-wing groups, to recognize the more subtle, but still very damaging ways in which key social institutions and structures – such as law, education, and the media – are racist, as well as patriarchal. We need to study whiteness as a privileged and socially constructed racial and political category, in the same way we have looked at masculinity. Academics Patricia Hill Collins and Angela Davis developed these ideas further, to look at how race, class, and sexuality affect our experience of gender.

I've got all my sisters with me

US author and academic bell hooks has argued that a problem with saying "I'm a feminist" is that it means you look at the world from a very individual viewpoint. But if you say "I support feminism", it encourages you to recognize a range of oppressions; womanism encourages this.

Womanist thinking is about how black women relate to each other and the world; it celebrates black sisterhood, heritage, friendships, and support systems. It looks at the impact of a working-class position, and sexuality. Although it fights sexism within the black community, womanism is not against black men – it recognizes their role in families and their shared experiences in a racist society. All this is poignantly portrayed in the novels of Toni Morrison, the first and, so far, only black woman to win the Nobel literature prize.

Womanism also asks why, to be represented politically or culturally, black women often have to settle for the choice between a black man or a white woman – as comedian Wanda Sykes said about the 2008 Democratic candidates: "I'm a black woman – Hillary or Obama, I'm torn". Just like feminism, womanism will mean and include different things for different women. Spreading from its US roots, today it has been taken up in various African countries and in black communities across Europe.

CHECK YOUR PRIVILEGE

In her 2014 blog "Why I no longer talk to white people about race", British writer Reni Eddo-Lodge points out how structural racism persists, and that part of the problem is when well-meaning white people, or those trying to be politically correct, ignore race rather than acknowledging their white privilege.

Relationships and FAMILIES

Female FRIENDSHIPS

Girls who like BOYS

GIRLS who like GIRLS

Happily MARRIED?

HAVING it all?

Raising GIRLS and BOYS

FAMILY values

An unfair DIVORCE

CONTROLLING your own BODY

No ALWAYS means NO

DOMESTIC violence

RECLAIM the NIGHT

Feminists put our intimate relationships under the spotlight, arguing that intensely personal aspects of our lives – our relationships with our families, with other girls, and with boys – are shaped by society. Second-wave feminists sought to liberate women from restrictive traditional relationship models, and today the fight continues to give women more marital, sexual, and reproductive choices.

Female
FRIENDSHIPS

Feminists in the late 1960s argued that "the personal is political". By this they meant that women's inequality affected them in every part of their lives. Feminists began to consider the importance of friendship in women's lives. Social scientists have shown that girls' and women's friendships are vital for social support.

Divide and conquer

In the view of American feminist Kate Millett, in her book *Sexual Politics*, women have been systematically isolated from one another, by being refused access to education, or being expected to stay at home after marriage. Other feminists have argued that girls and women are taught to view each other as competition. According to Nigerian feminist Chimamanda Ngozi Adichie "we raise girls to see each other as competitors... for the attention of men". This supports male dominance because if women are at odds with one another then they are more likely to be dependent on men. Girls are also taught that their friendships are fleeting and less significant than the intimate relationships they will later develop with boys and men. For example, British feminist Angela McRobbie has shown how teenage magazines for girls emphasize heterosexual romantic relationships as the ultimate goal for girls, at the expense of their friendships with other girls.

> In 1991, Harvard Medical School found that the more friends women have, the better their overall health.

IN GIRLS, OUT GIRLS

In 2003, Kimberly Scott's study "In Girl Out Girl and Always Black" looked at African American girls' friendships. It filled an important gap in research as most other studies had looked only at the friendships of white girls. She studied the intersections of gender and race in school and neighbourhood friendships, and how girls helped each other to navigate a world largely dominated by white men.

Sisterhood

Female friendships have always been important, but during the late 1960s and 1970s, with the rise of feminist activism, the idea of "sisterhood" asserted friendships as powerful and an important source of confidence for women. In the late 1960s women in the US formed groups for "consciousness-raising" – a form of activism where women could share their experiences and increase awareness of women's oppression. Research by American psychologist Cary Cherniss (1972), showed that friendships with other women were valuable in themselves, rather than being second best to their relationships with men. Cherniss

FRIENDS for LIFE

Mia, Anita, and Kim are best friends. They do everything together.

One day, Anita meets Jack. Mia and Kim are sad that they don't see Anita much anymore.

Then, Anita and Jack fall out. Anita is upset and tells her friends.

Luckily, Anita's friends are there for her, and their friendship gets stronger.

found that talking was a key aspect of friendship between women and related closely to an overall sense of wellbeing.

See also: 30-31, 130-131

It's different for girls?

More recent research has looked at the ways young girls are encouraged to scrutinize themselves and each other. English feminist Sue Lees observed this in British school playgrounds in the 1990s. In her book, *Sugar and Spice* (1993), Lees discussed how girls are encouraged to police other girls and comment on their looks and behaviours. American feminist Roxane Gay suggests that this behaviour isolates girls and women and supports male dominance, because it's hard to see another woman as an ally when you've been taught that she's your competition. Gay calls for women to "abandon the cultural myth that all female friendships must be bitchy, toxic, or competitive. This myth is like heels and purses – pretty but designed to slow women down".

Today, lots of friendships are formed and maintained online. Of course, the Internet, just like face-to-face interactions, has its dangers and it seems girls are particularly vulnerable to online bullying. The Cyberbullying Research Center has shown that up to 1 in 5 girls in the US will experience online abuse. Girls tend to "chat" more online and post pictures of themselves, which can put them at risk of gossip and shaming. However, the Internet has also provided girls with another place to form friendships, share interests, and build communities and support networks.

> ## "Friendship gives us the solidarity to get through the inconvenience, fear, confusion, and even danger of being female."
>
> Kate Leaver, *The Friendship Cure* (2018)

Girls who like BOYS

Today, most women are more empowered than ever before, but in social situations the expectations of gender roles still influence the balance of power between men and women. So, how do heterosexual women navigate relationships with men?

Questioning convention

Feminism has sometimes wrongly been portrayed as "man-hating", but feminists do not hate men, and many seek fulfilling heterosexual romantic relationships. But feminists have sought to make male and female relationships more equal. Throughout history many have criticized the traditional institution of marriage (see pp 74–75) and have reformed many of its restrictions (that were largely on women). However, UK feminists Stevi Jackson and Sue Scott have suggested

EMPOWERING BOYS

US author and educator Jackson Katz has worked to challenge traditional ideas about masculinity. He has spoken about the need for men and boys to have healthy relationships and runs programmes that aim to empower them to call out sexist behaviour.

BEING A FEMINIST DOES NOT HAVE TO MEAN GIVING UP RELATIONSHIPS WITH MEN

THE ROM

★ ★ ★ ★ ★

"ASTOUNDING!"

★ ★ ★ ★

that straight women should go further and question the very idea of marriage itself. They argue that the emphasis put on "the couple" as the dominant form of relationship, enforced by a patriarchal society, can have a negative effect on other relationships. For example, women may neglect relationships with friends and family, seeing these as less important. They believe that feminists should question the idea of a heterosexual relationship fulfilling all the needs of a woman's life.

See also: 14–15, 74–75, 90–91

COM FILM

★★★★★
"HILARIOUS!"
★★★★

Girl meets boy

Opposite-sex relationships are becoming more equal, but popular media, such as romantic comedies, still portray meeting "the one" as a crucial goal of a woman's life. Many depictions of relationships still show active men pursuing passive women and are very heteronormative (treating heterosexuality as the default or "normal" sexual orientation). Jackson argues that straight women should be aware that being heterosexual is a privileged position and they should use this to support women of other sexualities. While gay or bisexual women have to "come out", for straight women their sexuality is accepted right away.

Many elements of popular culture also present an unrealistic and sometimes damaging portrayal of heterosexual romantic love. A 2015 study even showed that watching romantic comedies can potentially make stalking seem romantic. Challenging these stereotypical romantic norms can allow men and women to find new ways to conduct relationships.

Reshaping relationships

Many organizations are working to help young people, both boys and girls, have healthier relationships with each other. UK sociologist Jessica Ringrose has studied how teenage girls reacted to being in a feminist "girl power" group. While she noted that it did give them a sense of empowerment over their own choices, the girls still bought into negative double standards about boys and girls' sexual behaviour. They saw girls as either slutty or non-slutty but didn't apply similar labels to the boys. Other campaigns have worked with boys to question ideas surrounding masculinity.

"Heterosexuality is not normal, it's just common."

Dorothy Parker, US author

GIRLS who like GIRLS

Feminists have long argued that female sexuality should be considered as important as male sexuality. But what does this mean for women who are interested in dating other women? Often facing both sexism and homophobia, lesbian and bisexual women have had their own set of struggles.

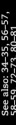
See also: 34–35, 56–57, 58–59, 72–73, 80–81

Double trouble

In a male-focused society, women who like women can be seen as a double threat – firstly because they go against the heterosexual "norm", and secondly as they demonstrate the fact that female sexuality does not only exist to serve the needs of men. Feminists such as US writer Adrienne Rich have shown how society has portrayed lesbians as deviant, sick, or sinful in order to uphold the notion of "compulsory heterosexuality" (see pp 34–35). Historically, many countries around the world have refused to acknowledge the existence of lesbianism, and it took famous legal cases such as the 1928 obscenity trials of English lesbian author Radclyffe Hall to bring it to public attention. Lesbians haven't always been criminalized in the same way gay men have, but they have faced homophobia and violence. Throughout history, lesbians have always played an important role in the women's movement.

> **"Give us also the right to our existence!"**
>
> **Radclyffe Hall, *The Well of Loneliness* (1928)**

Multiple identities

Women who identify as lesbians can express their identity in many ways. During the 20th century, terms like "butch" (usually meaning traditionally masculine in style and self-presentation) and "femme" (feminine in style) began to be used in lesbian subculture. Some feminists saw these labels as just replicating restrictive heterosexual gender roles, but others, such as US author Joan Nestle and US academic Anne Fausto-Sterling, have argued that all masculine and feminine gender identities are socially constructed – not some "natural" and others imitations. Therefore, butch and femme are unique forms of lesbian self-expression.

Not all women who like women are lesbians. Many may identify as bisexual, pansexual, or gender fluid and reject what they see as strict labels. Because of their often conventionally feminine appearance, femme lesbians and bisexual women have had problems getting their sexuality recognized. The terms "bi-invisibility" and "bi-erasure" were concepts developed by bisexuals in the 1990s who found the LGBTQ community didn't always see them as truly queer. But things are changing. Mainstream US girls' magazine *Teen Vogue* gives advice for how to avoid assuming heterosexuality is the default, and a 2017 survey from anti-bullying initiative Ditch the Label found that 57 per cent of teens sampled in the UK and US said they didn't fit into the traditional definition of heterosexuality.

JEWELLE GOMEZ

US author Jewelle Gomez explores many of the issues surrounding being an LGBTQ woman of colour in her work. Gomez (right) and her wife Diane Sabin (left) were part of the campaign for same-sex marriage in California, US, which was initially legalized in 2008 but then faced further legal challenges.

Pride and prejudice

The situation for same-sex couples continues to improve, and throughout the 2000s and 2010s many countries passed laws to allow same-sex marriage. Lesbian role models can be seen on TV, such as US actress, comic, and TV host Ellen DeGeneres, and actresses such as Lea de Laria and Ruby Rose have been cast in prominent lesbian roles. However, in the media, male gay relationships are still more visible than female ones. A 2017-18 survey showed that gay men make up the majority of regular LGBTQ characters (47 per cent) on TV shows, with lesbians making up just 24 per cent. Although prejudices still exist, increased visibility and activism is helping recognize and celebrate female same-sex relationships.

Judith Butler

Born 1956

American academic Judith Butler took part in shaping the "third wave" of feminism in the 1990s, which recognized that women have to deal with inequality not just based on being female, but also due to gender, race, and class barriers. Butler changed the way people thought about being male or female by saying that we do not have to be limited by either classification.

Queer theory

Judith Butler questions the binaries (systems made up of two categories) of gender and sexuality. These binaries suggest that a person is either masculine or feminine and straight or gay. Butler argues that gender and sexuality are not limited to these categories but are fluid and exist on a spectrum – in other words, we can have parts of both categories in our identity. These ideas about the nature of gender and sexuality break down the established links between sex, gender, and desire, and are part of what is known as "queer theory".

Performing gender

Butler suggests that ideas of what it means to be masculine or feminine are created by society, and our behaviour is influenced by what others expect from us. She calls the way we act, walk, and talk "performative acts", because we pick up behaviours and perform them like actors. Gender is therefore something we do rather than what we are. Masculinity and femininity are not natural but constructed by the way we act them out. Butler says "gender is an imitation for which there is no original".

Crossing boundaries

Those who don't conform to society's gender expectations are defined as marginal or deviant. Butler argues that these marginal identities can subvert gender norms. Performances that cross the boundaries of gender and sexuality, such as cross-dressing and drag, as well as butch-femme lesbian identities, help break down the gender binary because they show that gender is constructed and performed.

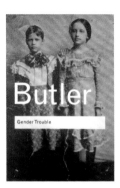

Gender trouble

Butler published *Gender Trouble: Feminism and the Subversion of Identity* in 1990. In this influential book, she proposed that gender is not something we are born as, but something we become through our everyday behaviour.

> **"Gender is culturally formed, but it is also a domain of agency or freedom."**

Speaking up

Judith Butler received a PhD in Philosophy from Yale University, US. She now teaches at the University of California, Berkeley, US, and gives lectures around the world.

Happily MARRIED?

While marriage rates in the US and Europe have been declining since the 1960s, marriage is still the norm. Most people still get married, although, these days, most people marry later than in previous generations, and lots of people marry more than once. If marriage is still the most common and approved family structure, is it a topic that feminists need to talk about?

What's yours is mine

Marriage has been a focus of feminist critique for centuries. English feminist Mary Astell warned women against it in the 18th century. She believed marriage, at the time, represented an unequal partnership that trapped women because they had no legal rights. It was very difficult for a woman to leave an unhappy or abusive marriage, and even if she succeeded, once separated she had no access to her children or her own earnings. This is because, until the late 19th century, women in England and the US were considered to be the property of their husbands, under the common law concept known as coverture. Although this is no longer the case in the West, some wedding traditions still reflect this view. In Christian ceremonies, the woman is walked down the aisle by her father, who then passes her over to her future husband. She then often takes her husband's surname.

> The average age of marriage has risen in every region of the world for both men and women.

Behind every good man...

In recent decades, marriage and the idea of the nuclear family, made up of a married heterosexual couple with children has been challenged, including by feminists. Historically, the expectation was that after marriage came a family, with care for both husband and children being the wife's responsibility. French feminist Christine Delphy saw marriage as a tool for men to control women's reproduction and unpaid labour, thus upholding male dominance. By taking care of the children, women enabled men to enter the workforce. This made a wife financially dependent on her husband, and meant that it was harder for her to leave if the marriage deteriorated.

Marriage equality

Feminists also argue that the institution of marriage is heteronormative – it promotes monogamous heterosexual relationships as the norm. For this reason LGBTQ activists disagree on the issue of gay marriage. Some want the right to marry, while others view marriage as designed to uphold outmoded social conventions.

> "I have yet to hear a man ask for advice on how to combine marriage and a career."
>
> Gloria Steinem (1984)

Fairytale romance

So why do so many people get married? American poet and feminist Adrienne Rich explained it in terms of persistent ideas about romantic love. Stories that end with a "happy ever after" are everywhere – in myths and fairytales, in films, books, and the media. American sociologist Ann Swidler argues, in her book *Talk of Love* (2001), that the ideal model of love persists because marriage, as an institution, requires it. Major religions endorse marriage, too, and key social

A CONTRACT

Christine Delphy argues that the marriage contract is a work contract, and a source of oppression. In a world where women are paid less than men and have limited access to positions of power, they are driven to marry for financial security. In return, men benefit from their labour in the home. It is a system that reproduces itself.

institutions support it, by rewarding those who marry, for example with tax advantages or cheaper insurance, and penalizing those who don't. Feminists suggest that society promotes marriage because it sustains male dominance and supports capitalism.

Modern marriages

Today, many places in Europe and the US recognize same-sex marriage or civil partnerships. Trends in marriage have changed, yet most people still get married. But many feminists, including Claudia Card in the US, have argued that marriage still benefits men more than it does women, for example when women take on the majority of housework and childcare. Studies have even shown that single women live longer than married women, while married men live longer than single ones.

WOMEN TODAY ARE CHALLENGING
THE TRADITIONAL VIEW OF MARRIAGE

See also: 32–33, 68–71, 76–77, 80–83, 106–107

HAVING it all?

The issue of work is complicated for many women once they decide to have children. The competing demands of family and career may force them to juggle their responsibilities in a way that men rarely have to.

A hard sell

In 1982, *Cosmopolitan* editor Helen Gurley Brown wrote *Having It All: Love, Success, Sex, Money... Even if You're Starting With Nothing.* Brown later said that the title wasn't her idea, but "having it all" – combining a career and motherhood – became the catchphrase for a generation. Today, the phrase is still used with irony by time-starved mothers as they juggle the demands of work with family life.

Loaded scales

In England, three-quarters of mothers with dependent children are now in full- or part-time work, according to the Office for National Statistics. The increasing numbers of working mothers can be explained by new childcare policies, flexible working practices, and – perhaps most importantly – the fact it often takes more than one wage to support a family. Work patterns in the West vary, but more than half of US families have two full-time earners, while in Germany 1.5 salaries are the norm.

Despite this trend, men have been slow to take up the slack in the home, with childcare and housework still falling largely to women (see pp 106–107). Women are also at a disadvantage because they are usually paid less than men, and work in in lower paid jobs. In her article "Making Motherhood Work" (2011), British sociologist Rachel Thomson states that the "motherhood penalty" is estimated to reduce women's pay by one-fifth. In turn this means that there is a certain logic for a woman to give up her job, rather than her better paid partner. Patriarchal societies have little interest in challenging this situation, which guarantees men the best-paid jobs, as well as an inbuilt family support network.

CAN WOMEN FIND A PERFECT BALANCE

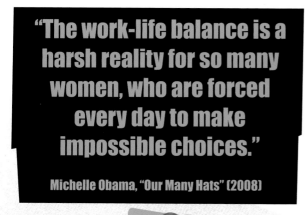

"The work-life balance is a harsh reality for so many women, who are forced every day to make impossible choices."

Michelle Obama, "Our Many Hats" (2008)

See also: 102–103, 106–107

Working at home

For many women, particularly those from low-income groups, work is a necessity, but some women find it is impossible to "have it all" and give up work. One study in the US found over 40 per cent of high-powered women now leave work to look after children. While some report this is because they can't reconcile maternal love with going out to work, others say that exhaustion prevents them from giving their all to a career, so they leave.

The feminist struggle for women's right to work outside the home has been criticized for devaluing work in it. However, feminists do recognize that domestic labour in the home is definitely work. The debate is around the fact that, because this work is unpaid, the woman is dependent on the wage-earner, and there is an imbalance of power in the partnership.

A shared responsibility

Both women who work and those who don't can suffer from guilt and frustration at their situation. Working women often feel they should be there more for family. Women who stay at home may feel they are falling short of their potential, or are unhappy being financially dependent on their partner.

Recognizing that "having it all" is impossible is perhaps the first step to peace of mind, but working towards a work-life balance that works for the whole family will only be achieved by breaking with stereotypes, giving men and women flexible work and equal pay, and sharing responsibility.

BETWEEN FAMILY LIFE AND WORK?

TRAPPED

US writer Betty Friedan, in her 1963 book *The Feminine Mystique*, said that women were trapped in the role of housewives, but didn't want to admit it for fear of appearing unfeminine. Her book became a bestseller, and played a key role in the 1960s feminist movement.

Raising GIRLS and BOYS

In a society that's rife with gender stereotypes, we are taught that boys and girls are inherently different – they have different needs, behaviours, and interests. Sayings such as "boys will be boys", "boys don't cry", and "daddy's little princess" reinforce our ideas about gender differences. But are boys and girls really that dissimilar?

Stereotypes at play

Ideas about gender difference start early. Children's nursery rhymes, stories, and fairy tales teach us that girls are passive princesses, twiddling their thumbs while they wait to be rescued. Boys, in contrast, are brave heroes, battling monsters on their way to rescue damsels in distress. Wander down the aisles of most toy and clothes shops and the story is very similar. Toys aimed at boys are often scientific or encourage boisterous outdoor play. Girls can expect toys, such as dolls, that encourage an interest in fashion, or even housework, presumably preparing them to be good wives and mothers. While girls are often comfortable playing with toys designed for boys, boys are very reluctant to play games considered to be "girly". So boys and girls both learn early on that society values "masculine" attributes more than those considered to be "feminine".

> Pink used to be a "boy colour" and blue a "girl colour". Before that, all babies wore white dresses.

The same underneath

Clothing also reflects supposed gender differences. Pink, flowery skirts for girls; blue, practical trousers for boys. Girls' clothes may be designed with fashion in mind, whereas clothes for boys are designed for practicality.

We are told so often that girls and boys are different that we assume these differences are natural and normal. However, feminists believe that far from being innate, gender stereotypes are created by society.

See also: 48–53, 56–57, 102–103

STEREOTYPES OF WHAT IT MEANS TO BE

"Boys and girls grow up in different cultures."

Lise Eliot, *Pink Brain, Blue Brain* (2009)

"Brave boys" and "gentle girls"

British sociologist Ann Oakley suggested in her book *Sex, Gender and Society* (1972) that we are taught how to be "normal" men and women from very early on, in a process called socialization. From an early age, children are learning what society expects of them through a whole range of cues. Some are obvious: for example, research suggests that children copy the gender roles of their parents. In families where one parent is the caregiver and the other the "breadwinner", their children are likely to mimic

EARLY LEARNING

American neuroscientist Lise Eliot has shown that people unconsciously treat babies differently depending on their sex. In research, girls were seen as more social than boys (even when they were in fact baby boys dressed up as girls). Despite their brains being very similar at birth, she argues, early learning and play steers girls and boys into gendered roles.

these roles in their own behaviour. But there are many more subtle ways in which children learn what behaviour is acceptable for boys or for girls, too. Caregivers have been observed to pay boys more attention if they are assertive and demanding, but respond to girls who speak or interact more gently. Girls are in this way rewarded for being passive communicators, and punished for being assertive or aggressive, while the opposite is true for boys.

Harmful stereotypes

Gender stereotypes are powerful, and can be damaging when they limit children's choices, or stop them from doing what they might be good at. If cultural expectations teach us that girls and boys should behave in a certain way, or have certain likes or dislikes, then a child whose personality doesn't fit that mould may struggle to fit in.

In recent years, there has been a growing awareness of the impact of gendered toys and clothes in childhood. In the UK, campaigns such as Pink Stinks and Let Toys Be Toys have lobbied manufacturers and retailers to stop aiming certain toys at boys and others at girls. In 2017, high-street retailer John Lewis announced it would no longer label its clothes as being "for boys" or "for girls". The aim is to let children decide what they like, free from cultural expectations.

A MAN OR WOMAN BEGIN IN CHILDHOOD

FAMILY values

Following improvements to women's rights in the 20th century, family structures began to change. Social trends such as people choosing to marry later in life (or not at all), an increase in the number of divorces, and a growing number of official same-sex couples, means that cultural ideas about what a family is have changed.

See also: 68–69, 70–71, 74–75, 76–77, 84–85

A perfect family?

Fifty years ago, the most common family structure in the West, known as the nuclear family, consisted of a husband and wife with children. American sociologist Talcott Parsons saw this type of family as one of the building blocks of society, a safe place where children could learn social values. However, feminists argued that this traditional family structure was oppressive to women because it relied on gender roles that confined women to the home and excluded them from the workforce,

entrenching gender inequality. French feminist Christine Delphy argued that wives were exploited in family set-ups, through unpaid labour in the home and their related economic dependence on their husbands. Parsons also failed to recognize that his idealized model family was only relevant for a minority of (mostly) white, middle-class, heterosexual couples. Other family forms have always existed, but they were not considered to be as desirable or stable as the nuclear family, an idea that has since been rejected.

Single person

In 2015, same-sex marriages accounted for 2.6 per cent of all marriages that took place in the UK.

Inter-racial family

Couple without children

Blended family

Same-sex inter-racial couple with children

FAMILIES IN THE WEST NOW COME IN ALL DIFFERENT SHAPES AND SIZES

Brave new family

The late 20th-century expansion of capitalism saw unemployment and poverty rise. This, in addition to changing attitudes and laws on divorce, caused the family to undergo a radical shift, according to American sociologist Judith Stacey. Views of men as breadwinners and women as housewives became less prevalent. Changes in women's rights gave women the freedom to delay marriage and pursue education and employment, a change also made possible by the introduction of birth control.

> **"Western family arrangements are diverse, fluid, and unresolved."**
>
> **Judith Stacey, *In the Name of the Family* (1996)**

The "postmodern" family

Divorce may have risen across Europe and the US from the 1970s (although it's now declining again) but it seems there is still a commitment to the social ties of love. People continue to want to experience family life through new dynamics of remarriage or cohabitation. Marrying again commonly results in "blended" or "reconstituted" families, where children live with a step-parent and step-siblings.

   Another increasingly common family structure is the single-parent family. Single mothers have been given a bad press in the past, but more recently society has recognized that women choosing to have a child on their own, through adoption or donor conception, can be a positive decision. Changes in laws also mean that gay and lesbian couples have become more visible in many Western societies, and research shows that children of same-sex parents thrive socially and academically. While family life takes many different forms, most people still choose to have some kind of long-term relationship with a partner, and frequently with children. Family structures might be changing, but people continue to choose family life, in one of many forms.

Lesbian couple

Gay parents

Family with older parents

One-parent family

LESBIAN ADOPTION

Though single women (and men) in the UK have been able to adopt, regardless of their sexual orientation, since the 1920s, it took until 2005 for lesbian and gay couples to have the same right. Since then the number of adoptions by same-sex couples has steadily increased, now accounting for around 10 per cent of adoptions.

An unfair
DIVORCE

Today, we may take it for granted that anyone in an unhappy marriage should have the right to divorce. But this wasn't always the case. Until the 1960s, it was rare and frowned upon. In most parts of the world it is now easier to divorce, but many women find themselves worse off afterwards than their former husbands.

See also: 14–15, 74–75, 76–77

Till death us do part

Marriage is often presented as the most important of relationships, and the goal of every little girl. First-wave feminists challenged the idea of marriage by showing how marriage and the termination of marriage are controlled by the patriarchal state (see pp 74–75).

For many married couples, divorce used to be something that only men could initiate, and in some countries it still is. US law professor Katharine Bartlett highlights how man's "absolute tyranny" over women in marriage was a reason for women to seek suffrage. Until the 19th century in many countries, a wife's property became her husband's when they married, as did her labour, her body, and their children – so after divorce she'd often be left with nothing and be shunned by society. Some early feminists, such as American suffragist Elizabeth Cady Stanton, argued for divorce to be made more available

to women, but other pro-marriage suffragists feared divorce as women had so much to lose. Even after women gained the right to own property, it was hard for women

FINANCIAL DISADVANTAGE CAN BE A BARRIER FOR WOMEN WHO WANT A DIVORCE

to get a divorce – they had to prove their marriage had serious faults and would have no claim on anything their husband had made during marriage, despite the fact their work in the home had enabled their husband's career.

Should I stay or should I go?

In the 1970s, the National Organization for Women (NOW), led by American writer Betty Friedan, campaigned for economic protection for women and children, such as the equal division of property, to be introduced alongside no-fault divorce reforms in the US. Despite divorce settlements in many countries recognizing the value of a wife's work within marriage since the 1970s, many women end up worse off financially

TRIPLE TALAQ

Until 2017, in India a man could end his marriage simply by saying *talaq*, meaning "divorce", to his wife three times. The Indian supreme court ruled "triple talaq" unconstitutional, after the Indian Muslim Women's Movement, co-founded by Zakia Soman (pictured), campaigned against it.

than their husbands. Whilst more women now work, many still take time out of their career to raise children, so after divorcing they may re-enter the workplace at a financial disadvantage – especially when, typically, women receive unequal pay. A divorced woman will often be granted custody of the children, so will need to find childcare if she does work, making her still dependent on her ex-husband for financial support.

Whilst significant progress has been made around the world, in some countries there is still a long way to go. In Egypt, men are able to divorce their wives without going through the courts, but women cannot. A woman who wants to leave her husband must give up her financial rights, creating a barrier for many women. In other countries, such as Malta and the Philippines, divorce remains illegal for most people under their country's laws.

"For women to have full human identity and freedom, they must have economic independence."

Betty Friedan, "Up from the kitchen floor" (1973)

CONTROLLING your own BODY

The fight for reproductive rights – giving women control over when or if they have children – has been central to feminist activism for many years. Feminists have argued that women around the world need access to family planning resources to truly have control over both their bodies and their lives.

Preventing pregnancy

Feminists argue that women should be free to protect themselves from unplanned pregnancies. After all, it is the female body that must take the toll of pregnancy and childbirth, and a woman is also likely to bear more responsibility in raising a child than a man. Although women have used natural contraceptives, such as plants, for thousands of years, these were often crude and unhygienic, and frowned upon by society. Modern, reliable, and safe birth control began to become available only at the start of the 20th century – when feminist pioneers such as Marie Stopes in the UK and Margaret Sanger in the US founded the first clinics to give women access to it. Often hailed as a landmark medical breakthrough for women, the contraceptive pill was introduced in the 1960s, and other advances later followed.

Reproductive freedom?

Birth control has often faced opposition from religious groups and in many countries, such as Pakistan and Zimbabwe, it is still very difficult for women to access. Around the world, 214 million women have an unmet need for contraception, with most of these located in parts of Africa and Southeast Asia. Although birth control provision is generally better in parts of Europe and North and South America, some women may only have the option of

permanent measures such as sterilization, and little access to reversible methods. Other women may still need a doctor's permission to access these.

In places where it is more widely available, birth control can claim some impressive achievements. In the US, studies have shown that women who have access to contraception are significantly more likely to go on to higher education. Greater access to birth control would also help women in the developing world,

See also: 30–31, 106–107

FGM

Somalian-born author Hibo Wardere campaigns to raise awareness about FGM (female genital mutilation), a traditional practice in some parts of Africa, Asia, and the Middle East. More than 200 million girls and women have experienced this removal or cutting of their external genitalia, which can often lead to lifelong pain and damage.

allowing many to have bigger gaps between children, which has been shown to improve the health and survival rates of both mothers and infants.

Access to abortion

Contraception is not foolproof, so many feminists have argued that access to abortion is also essential. This, however, is highly contested across the globe. In many nations, due to laws or religious beliefs, abortions are illegal, sometimes even in cases of rape. Not all feminists agree either – some believe the rights of a woman's unborn child take precedence over her right to control her body. But, where women are prevented from legal abortion, illegal, unsafe abortions still take place – causing around 70,000 maternal deaths annually. Protests over abortion have taken place around the world. Using slogans such as "my body, my choice", many women have argued that (largely male) lawmakers should not able to force a woman to carry a child. Laws are still changing today. In 2018, after decades of feminist campaigning, the law outlawing abortion in Ireland was overturned by a massive popular vote – a victory that brought together people from all walks of life.

The road ahead

As feminist activism continues, gradually women have gained more reproductive choices in more countries. Feminists are also pushing for research to reduce the side-effects of some birth control methods, and also into male contraceptives so that the burden of preventing pregnancy does not fall on women alone.

> **"No woman can call herself free who does not own and control her body."**
>
> Margaret Sanger, US birth control activist and Founder of Planned Parenthood

FEMINISTS HAVE CAMPAIGNED FOR WOMEN'S RIGHT TO A RANGE OF REPRODUCTIVE CHOICES

Frida Kahlo

1907–1954

She may have died more than 50 years ago, but the image of Mexican artist Frida Kahlo lives on as a symbol of women's liberation. She did not allow the fact that she was a woman, or that she had a disability, to limit her. She is admired for her uncompromising art, her distinctive fashion style, and her social activism. Her home in Mexico City is now a museum, and her paintings feature in exhibitions worldwide.

> **"I am my own muse, I am the subject I know best. The subject I want to know better."**

Sense of self

Although Frida Kahlo did not take part in the women's rights movement, today she is considered a feminist icon. Many of Kahlo's paintings explore female sexuality, menstruation, miscarriage, and abortion – topics that were considered taboo in the 1920s and 1930s. Despite living in a conservative Catholic society, where women were not supposed to stand out, Frida Kahlo did not follow social conventions. She married artist Diego Rivera, but had relationships with other men, as well as women.

Overcoming suffering

At the age of six, Kahlo contracted polio, which meant that one of her legs became weaker and thinner. Her father encouraged her to be strong and active, and she learnt to play sports and dance. Bright at school, she was planning a career in medicine when a bus accident at the age of 18 left her virtually crippled. Forced to stay in bed for months with most of her body in a cast, she began to paint images of herself and her injured body.

A fairer society

Because of her injuries, Kahlo had numerous operations and was unable to have children. Her paintings often show her personal pain. Many can also be interpreted as expressing the pain of her country, which had suffered for centuries after the Spanish colonized Mexico and became its ruling class. Kahlo spoke out against the wealthy, powerful elite, joining the Communist Party at the age of 15 to fight injustice.

Iconic look
Dressing in the long skirts worn by native Mexican women, and using Aztec symbolism in her art, Frida Kahlo promoted indigenous folk culture at a time when it was not valued or respected by society.

Pain and beauty
In this self-portrait, painted in 1940, the pretty flowers and unique earrings (given to her by Picasso) contrast strongly with the piercing wreath of thorns around her neck, symbolizing her constant pain.

No ALWAYS means NO

Feminists have attempted to expose the levels of violence in women's lives for centuries but have faced many hurdles. With an increase in high profile rape and sexual assault cases in recent years across the media worldwide, a spotlight has been shone on sexual violence and those fighting to stop it.

Everyday violence

Experiences of rape and sexual harassment are a feature of daily life for many women and girls around the world. According to UN Women, 120 million girls worldwide have experienced forced sex or other sexual acts, and it is estimated that 35 per cent of all women will experience sexual violence in their lifetime. While there are a growing number of initiatives that support victims of sexual violence, this type of crime remains under-reported – in the US in 2016, only 23 per cent of incidences of rape or sexual assault were reported to the police, and in India in 2002, as few as eight per cent of victims sought help. Feminists have argued that sexual assault happens as a result of gender inequality and also helps to maintain this inequality. Susan Brownmiller, an American writer, argued that society's model of masculinity, which rewards male aggression and power imbalances between the sexes, promotes a "rape culture" where women fear rape and men benefit from the control brought by that fear.

MOMENT OF TRUTH

Ujamaa, a charity in Kenya, aims to reduce incidences of rape by focusing on prevention. As well as educating girls on verbal and physical self-defence, Ujamaa provides lessons to boys called "Your Moment of Truth", which teaches them how to intervene if they witness violence against women and girls.

Power of myth

Persistent myths about rape and assault don't help. The perceptions that rapists are "strangers in dark alleys" and that women are somehow to blame when out alone, drinking alcohol, flirting, or wearing revealing clothing are alarmingly common. The media often concentrates on victims' behaviour and rarely focuses on the rapist – he becomes invisible or excused. In past cases of child sexual abuse, girls have been accused of being flirtatious or untrustworthy. The stereotype of male sexuality as aggressive and uncontrollable adds to this. American essayist Adrienne Rich called this the myth of the "overpowering, all-conquering sex drive" (1980). Myths and misconceptions can make it difficult to bring rape cases to trial. When a case pits one

A WOMAN'S BODY BELONGS TO HER AND HER ALONE

NO!

"We must send a message... that there is no disgrace in being a survivor of sexual violence; that the shame is on the aggressor."

Angelina Jolie, Global Summit to End Sexual Violence in Conflict (2014)

person's version of events against another's and victims feel that they will not be believed or were partially responsible for what happened, the majority of cases never get reported to the police. In many countries, women must prove they did not give consent (that they said or implied no) but this can be difficult if courts are led to think they are deceitful or responsible for what happened to them.

Changing minds, changing times

Things are slowly changing. In July 2018, Sweden introduced a new law that regards sex without explicit consent as rape, shifting the burden of proof from the victim to the accused – rather than a victim having to prove they said no, the accused must prove they gained consent. Many countries now have rape crisis centres and support lines and, often with help from organizations such as the United Nations and the World Health Organization, are taking the sexual abuse of children more seriously by increasing the age of consent and cracking down on child marriage. Historically, sex in a marriage was considered a marital right and non-consensual sex between a married couple was not illegal, but legislation around marital rape means that it is now a crime in many countries.

High profile rape cases have encouraged discussion around the issue of consent. Feminists argue that we need better sex and relationship education to make people aware that consent has to be made clear, people can change their mind at any point, alcohol and drugs affect a person's ability to give consent, and, most importantly, no always means no.

See also: 40–41, 90–91, 92–93

RECLAIM the NIGHT

Women first started marching through cities in torchlit night-time processions in the 1970s to "reclaim the night". They are still marching today, to demand the right for women to feel safe on the streets at night and to protest wider issues of violence against women.

Taking back the night

Inspired by a night-time march held in Brussels in 1976 to protest against crimes against women, the women of Rome and Berlin took to the streets in 1977 to "take back the night". These women felt unsafe after dark following a reported rise in rapes. Their protests struck a chord with feminists around West Germany and in Britain and the US, who coordinated processions of women with flaming torches through the darkness, demanding the right to walk alone at night without fear. Women were enraged by police advice to stay indoors for safety – a form of curfew.

Unsafe streets?

A 2005 survey in British teen magazine *More!* found that 95 per cent of women felt unsafe on streets at night. In fact, men are more likely to be victims of assault on the street. Why, then, is it women who are most afraid in public spaces, especially at night? British feminist academic Liz Kelly argues that common myths about rape contribute to women feeling more vulnerable. For example, many people think of rape as a crime committed by a stranger lurking in a dark alley.

MANY WOMEN FEEL UNSAFE WHEN THEY GO OUT AT NIGHT

In reality, women are more often raped by people they know, in places where they feel safe. In Europe and the US, fewer than 30 per cent of such attacks are committed by someone unknown to the victim.

Victim blaming?

If a woman is attacked at night, authorities often advise women and girls not to go out after dark. In 2017, police in Malmö, Sweden, issued this advice after a number of violent assaults against women and girls. This sparked angry protests and the police later formally retracted their statement. Similarly, following a series of assaults on female students on college campuses in the US in 2014, the campus police at the University of Wisconsin advised girls to modify their behaviour to avoid attack. They emailed safety tips to students including, "If you present yourself as easy prey, then expect to attract some wolves". In other words, women are held responsible for the violence against them.

Still marching

Attitudes towards responsibility for sexual violence are slowly changing. However, annual Reclaim the Night marches still take place around the world (under the banner of Take Back the Night in the US) to demand the right to use public space without fear and highlight the wider issues of violence against women and girls.

"No curfew on women – curfew on men."

Slogan from the first Reclaim the Night march (1977)

SLUT WALKS

In 2011, a police officer in Toronto, Canada, advised that "women should avoid dressing like sluts" to escape attack. In protest at this victim blaming and so-called "slut-shaming", women started protesting in their underwear to make a defiant display and reclaim the word "slut".

See also: 40–41, 88–89, 90–91, 134–135, 138–139

EDUCATION and WORK

An EQUAL EDUCATION?

WORK matters

WOMEN'S jobs, MEN'S jobs?

Doing it ALL

Gender PAY GAP

Is LANGUAGE man-made?

What is MANSPLAINING?

Women IN CHARGE

In education and employment, women and girls should be free to fulfil their full potential. Feminists have highlighted some of the issues still holding women back – from gender bias in the classroom to unequal pay and sexist attitudes at work. Feminists want to break down these barriers and increase women's representation in leadership roles and positions of political power.

An EQUAL EDUCATION?

In large parts of the world, it may feel like the battle for equal education for girls has already been won. In many countries, girls are now outperforming boys. But is their education now truly equal, or does gender bias in the classroom still influence the educational choices girls make?

Teacher's pets

From a young age, boys and girls are treated differently in the classroom. US researchers Myra Sadker, David Sadker, and Karen R. Zittleman logged thousands of hours in schools and found that teachers often pay far more attention to boys. They observed that teachers spend nearly two-thirds of their time talking with boys, praising and encouraging them more than girls. Teachers were also more likely to interrupt girls while letting boys talk over them.

Gender bias

These classroom interactions do not exist in a vacuum. They reinforce the gender stereotypes children already encounter in the media, and steer girls and boys into gender roles from an early age. Girls are praised for being neat, quiet, and calm, whereas boys are encouraged to be independent, active, and speak up. Anti-feminist campaigners often cite the fact that most teachers are female as something that disadvantages boys, but studies have shown that educators of both genders subconsciously treat boys

EDUCATION

STEM

22 + 56 = 78

BIAS IN THE WAYS GIRLS AND BOYS ARE TAUGHT MAY

> **"Education isn't simply about literacy, it's about giving girls back their power."**
>
> Shiza Shahid, Co-founder of the Malala Fund (2013)

more favourably. US researchers noted that when students didn't put their names on maths tests, girls scored higher than boys. But with recognizable "boy" or "girl" names written on the same tests, boys got higher scores. Racial biases can also influence educators. In the US, boys are more likely to be suspended than girls overall, but black girls are suspended at twice the rate of white boys, and far more than other girls.

STEM subjects

One of the key ways classroom bias may affect girls is in the gap in confidence seen between male and female students in some subjects. OECD (Organization for Economic Cooperation and Development) data from around the world showed that in all but three countries girls were far more likely to say they felt "helpless while performing a math problem", despite the fact their actual ability closely matched that of the boys.

SINGLE-SEX SCHOOLS

Single-sex schools are often suggested as a way to improve the academic performance of both girls and boys, although there is no firm evidence to support this. However, studies across English-speaking countries have shown that they can increase girls' take-up of traditionally male-dominated subjects.

See also: 16–17, 78–79, 102–103

INFLUENCE WHICH SCHOOL SUBJECTS THEY CHOOSE

When students choose which subjects to study, boys are more likely to choose STEM (science, technology, engineering, and maths) classes. Girls' preferences tend to be for English, biology, and languages. It could be that boys are encouraged to choose "masculine" STEM subjects and girls are steered towards the arts, but confidence may also play a part. Interestingly, it is countries with lower gender equality overall that end up with more female STEM graduates. Researchers have suggested this may be due to greater pressure to get a high-income job in order to escape inequality.

Promoting non-biased gender-neutral teaching in schools would encourage both girls and boys to follow their interests without feeling pressured into gendered routes. It may also lead to more girls taking up STEM careers, and help to get rid of bias in these fields.

Malala Yousafzai

Born 1997

Campaigning for the right of girls to be educated has made Malala Yousafzai the most famous young feminist in the world. She has been speaking out on the subject since she was 11, when the Taliban in her home province, in northwest Pakistan, attempted to stop girls going to school. She defied them – and their attempt to assassinate her – to become an activist, lobbying international organizations to champion youth education.

> **"Let us pick up our books and our pens. They are our most powerful weapons."**

Girls' right to learn

Malala's home in Pakistan's Swat Valley is a stronghold for the militant Taliban movement. They claim it "un-Islamic" for girls to attend school, and introduced a ban in 2008. The Pakistani government did not support the ban, but more than 80,000 girls stopped going to school. Determined to fight for the right to an education, Malala gave talks, wrote a blog for the BBC, and featured in a US documentary. Afraid of her growing influence, in 2012 the Taliban sent a gunman to kill her. She was shot in the head, neck, and shoulder.

Nobel Peace Prize

After undergoing life-saving surgery in Birmingham, UK, Malala made a full recovery. Refusing to be silenced, she became a global spokesperson for youth rights. In 2014, at the age of 17, she became the youngest person to win the Nobel Peace Prize, an honour she shared with Indian activist Kailash Satyarthi, "for their struggle against the suppression of children and young people and for the right of all children to education".

Malala Fund

Malala has used her fame to start a charity, which builds schools for girls in countries such as Nigeria and Syria, where education for women is often sidelined. To raise awareness for her cause she has met with world leaders, been on television, and become a spokesperson for the UN. Her own education continues at Oxford University, in the UK, where she studies philosophy, politics, and economics.

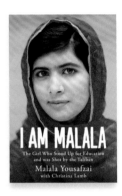

Her story
In 2013, she co-wrote *I Am Malala: The Girl Who Stood Up for Education and Was Shot by the Taliban*. Translated into more than 40 languages, it is a global bestseller.

Spreading word
Malala has shared her experiences, and her belief in the right of girls to get an education, across the world. Here she speaks to girls in a refugee centre in Kenya, in 2016.

WORK matters

Today, women make up at least 40 per cent of the workforce in more than 80 countries. For many women, work can be liberating – allowing them to earn, learn, contribute, create, and connect – as well as providing them with the financial independence to make decisions about their own lives.

Labour force

Women have always worked. In her book *If Women Counted* (1988) New Zealand feminist Marilyn Waring highlighted how women's unpaid work was essential to every country's economy, but remained largely invisible and unrecognized. Historically, more paid work was done by poorer women, and women were often underpaid, faced bad working conditions, and were barred from certain kinds of work. But many took action to change this. In the US, aspiring stockbroker Mary Gage started her own stock exchange for women in 1880, after being unable to trade with men. Women have also been active in trade unions – UK feminist Clementina Black helped found a trade union for women in the 19th century and UK activist Jessie Eden led working-class women on strikes in the 1920s and 1930s. In South Africa, women such as Frances Baard and Lilian Ngoyi fought for workers rights for oppressed black women during apartheid (enforced racial segregation).

> **"In the future, there will be no female leaders. There will just be leaders."**
>
> **Sheryl Sandberg, Lean In: Women, Work, and the Will to Lead (2013)**

WORK CAN ALLOW WOMEN TO USE THEIR

Leading the way

Today, there are many high-profile women in business, such as US businesswoman Sheryl Sandberg, who holds the role of Chief Operating Officer of technology company Facebook. In 2013, she wrote *Lean In*, a book of advice for women in business, although some feminists criticized its narrative as offering advice on how to succeed only by being more like men, rather

MICROFINANCE

Microfinance has helped many women in developing countries start their own businesses. It involves small loans that are given to people, women in particular, who wouldn't otherwise be able to get credit. These have helped many women in vulnerable circumstances create a livelihood for themselves.

than questioning the structure that advantages men in the first place. Women are also increasingly starting their own businesses. In 2016, around 163 million women across 74 countries worldwide were starting or running new businesses. As well as utilizing technology, women entrepreneurs often have sought to address women's issues in their ventures. In Uganda, entrepreneur Nanyombi Margaret Pearl runs a business that allows women to self-test for a vaginal infection. Samoan businesswoman Angelica Salele makes affordable, sustainable and reusable sanitary products for women across the Pacific islands.

Breadwinners

Women across the world are now more likely than ever before to be financially responsible for themselves and their families. Nearly 4 in 10 women in the US are primary breadwinners. Working women are also good for the economy. A study by the McKinsey Global Institute projects that if all women participated in the economy at the same rate as men, around $28 trillion dollars could be added to the global GDP (the value of all the goods and services produced).

See also: 102–103, 106–107, 108–109

SKILLS TO GAIN THE LIFESTYLE THEY WANT

WOMEN's jobs, MEN's jobs?

What do you want to be when you grow up? Following your dream should depend on your skills, intelligence, and strengths. But more often than not, jobs are divided by gender. People don't just have stereotypes about men and women, they stereotype jobs, too, assuming that men are a better fit for some jobs while women are more suited to others.

See also: 78–79, 100–101

Jobs for the boys (and girls)

Why do jobs get split into blue collar and pink collar work? A recent list of the 10 most female-dominated professions included primary school teachers, nurses, and secretaries. The most male-dominated jobs included construction workers, truck drivers, and software developers. With all the positive changes made over recent decades, and the creation of laws to prevent discrimination in the workplace, how did we end up here? Do men and women really have different skills and aptitudes that are suited to different jobs? A 2016 University of Toronto study did indicate that male and female workers may have some different strengths that suit them to specific jobs, such as faster reaction times in men, or greater manual dexterity in women. However, feminists argue that this alone does not account for the divide.

Mind the gap

The problem with this "occupational segregation" is that men's work and women's work are valued differently. American women typically earn 80 cents for every dollar that men are paid. However, this does not necessarily mean that women are doing the same work for less money. Rather, the fields of work dominated by women are not as highly valued, and therefore the jobs women do are often paid far less than the jobs that men do, even when they require a similar level of education. For example, the median earnings of information technology managers (mostly men) are 27 per cent higher than human resources managers (mostly women), according to Bureau of Labor Statistics data.

Finding a balance

For a long time, this gender pay gap (see pp.108–109) was dismissed by the observation that women simply chose to work in lower paying jobs, such as teaching and social work. However, a 2016 study by Cornell

EMOTIONAL LABOUR

In her 1983 book *The Managed Heart*, American sociologist Arlie Hochschild explored the idea that some jobs involve "emotional labour" – where workers must hide emotions or portray false emotions. Many jobs that require this, such as flight attendants, are dominated by women, and feminists have argued that women do the bulk of this unrecognized work.

University in New York, US, found that pay increases when men enter a field of work, even though the duties stay the same. For example, computer programming was a field developed by women and considered to be a woman's career as late as the 1960s. At the time it was low-paid and considered low status; however, today, computer programmers receive high salaries and they are now also mostly men. Conversely, the opposite effect happens when women enter "male" jobs – overall earnings decline.

In order to narrow the pay gap, we need a more equal workforce. Many initiatives have been launched to encourage more women into high-status male-dominated jobs, but this is only half the battle. The jobs women typically do also need to become valued more highly, especially as professions involving a caring element are likely to become increasingly important as more societies end up with aging populations. Getting rid of gender stereotypes about who can do which roles would help all industries recruit the best worker for the job – female or male.

> **"If they don't give you a seat at the table, bring a folding chair."**
>
> Shirley Chisholm, first African American Congresswoman

REMOVING GENDER STEREOTYPES WELCOMES MEN AND WOMEN INTO ALL JOBS

Audre Lorde

1934–1992

Audre Lorde once described herself as "black, lesbian, mother, warrior, poet", and since her death from breast cancer in 1992, she has been remembered as all of these things through her legacy of fiercely worded prose and poetry. Lorde used her gift for writing powerful and expressive verse to fight against sexism, racism, and homophobia.

> **"I am not free while any woman is unfree, even when her shackles are very different from my own."**

Speaking in poems

While growing up in New York, US, Audre Lorde became fascinated by poetry. She would recite her favourite lines in place of regular conversation. When she couldn't find existing poems that captured her feelings, she began to write her own. Her first published poem appeared in *Seventeen* magazine in 1951, but it was decades later that her poetry began to make a real impact.

Words as weapons

As a black, lesbian feminist, Lorde developed the point of view that "in our work and in our living, we must recognize that difference is a reason for celebration and growth, rather than a reason for destruction." She was involved in many political movements, including second-wave feminism, civil rights, and queer rights, and she used her poems as weapons to target prejudice. Her opinions about racism and class prejudice contributed to the evolution of feminist theory in the 1980s, which had up until then revolved mostly around the experiences of white, middle-class, straight women.

Fighting breast cancer

In her book *The Cancer Journals* (1989), Lorde wrote about her decade-long battle with breast cancer and how she coped after a mastectomy. She accused society of keeping quiet about her cancer, and encouraged women to speak out about their experiences, and to find strength in sharing their stories of survival.

Around the same time, Lorde co-founded Kitchen Table: Women of Color Press, a publishing house that was dedicated to promoting writing by black feminists.

The Audre Lorde Project
Founded in 1994, the Audre Lorde Project is a community organization in New York City to help people of colour who are lesbian, gay, bisexual, two spirit, transgender, and gender non-conforming. Activist Cara Page is seen here receiving an award on the project's behalf.

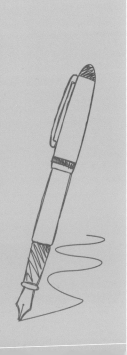

Inspirational teacher
Lorde, seen here in 1983, was a Master Artist in Residence at the Atlantic Center for the Arts in New Smyrna Beach, Florida.

Women are
power ful
dangerous

Doing it ALL

Today in the West, more women are working in paid employment outside the home than ever before, yet they are still doing the lion's share of housework. A 2018 UN report found that women do 2.6 times more unpaid caring and domestic work than men.

See also: 80–81, 102–103, 108–109

The second shift

In 1965, a US study showed that women spent nearly all their time doing unpaid housework. Men barely contributed. Today, many women have full-time jobs, but still take on the majority of the housework and childcare. A 2017 study showed that women consistently did more housework than men, regardless of career or income. Across the globe, women spend an average of 4.5 hours a day on unpaid work – more than double the amount men do. US sociologist Arlie Russell Hochschild referred to this as the "second shift" – unpaid labour women do when they have already done a day's work.

A woman's work is in the home

For much of history, a woman's place has been considered to be at home, but before the Industrial Revolution of the 19th century for many people the home was also the place where they generated their income - be it a farm or a workshop – so men and women largely worked alongside each other.

SOCIALIZED CHILDCARE

In 1920, Russian revolutionary Alexandra Kollontai argued that in order to achieve equality between the sexes, housework and childcare should not be women's duty, but should be paid for by the state. She argued that both men and women should work for, and be supported by, society, which should feed, bring up, and educate their children.

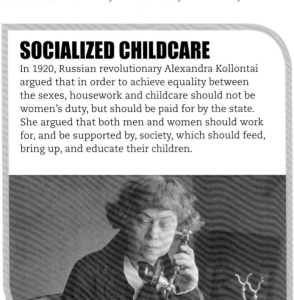

MANY WOMEN JUGGLE PAID WORK AND

The tasks they took on may have been different, but both were considered to be doing valuable labour. The gender split widened with industrialization, when paid work moved outside the home and into factories. Men assumed the role of "breadwinners", while women continued to work at home. Their unpaid work came to be seen as less valuable. Although some women worked in industry, such as in textile mills, they were paid less because they were not perceived as the principal earner of the household.

This arrangement suited both men and the economy. Women became free carers and family support workers, but also a flexible labour force. This was demonstrated during both World Wars, when women were called upon in vast numbers to work in weapons factories, on the land, and in support of the armed forces, but were promptly dismissed when the war ended and their jobs returned to men (see pp 26–27).

UNPAID FAMILY SUPPORT WORK

> ## "We are always their indispensable workforce."
>
> **Selma James, US social activist (1975)**

Wages for housework

While feminists must account for diverse relationships and not simply assume that all families consist of a heterosexual couple with children, getting recognition for the unpaid work that women do is a key issue for feminism. In 1972, an international campaign that began in Italy, called Wages for Housework, promoted the idea that the state should pay women for the work they do in the home. Italian Marxist Silvia Federici argued that this work gave an individual a role in society and that presenting it as a "natural attribute" of women means that it is often undervalued. Federici argues that this work needs to be seen as valuable and, to achieve this, women should demand a fair wage for domestic work, childcare, and even sex, to revolutionize the way we see and value this type of work and to benefit the whole working class.

Unequal opportunities

Many feminists disagree with Federici's ideas, since paying women for housework and caring responsibilities does not address the sexual division of this labour. Housework benefits everyone in a family, not just women, and can be isolating and unrewarding. The second shift also results in a time poverty gap between men and women that is clearly unfair – women who take on more tasks at home than their male partners have less time for themselves and, as a result, fewer opportunities to improve their education and career. Domestic labour should be valued and employers should offer flexible working hours to accommodate working parents, but ultimately the answer is for couples to share housework and other roles in their relationships equally.

Gender PAY GAP

Women make up half the world's potential talent pool. Unfortunately, their incomes are still at the shallow end. The gender pay gap exists in the majority of countries and in almost every field of work. Not only are men's incomes rising faster than women's, the gap is widening for the first time in a decade.

Latitudes and attitudes

Since 2006, the World Economic Forum (WEF) has collected data each year on the global gender gap. Its 2017 report compared information on gender equality from 144 countries. While gaps in educational attainment were closing, the economic gap was widening – despite initiatives such as making employers disclose their pay gaps. The WEF found that the average global pay for women in 2017 was $12,000 compared to $21,000 for a man. The extent of the pay gap varies globally. The hot spots for gender parity tend to be the smaller Western European countries, while the gap is most noticeable in the Middle East.

The pay gap for women in their 20s has been widening again after years of decline.

Women may fall into the "motherhood gap" if they opt to work flexibly around children.

WOMEN'S GAINS IN EDUCATION HAVE RESULTED IN ONLY SMALL IMPROVEMENTS IN PAY EQUITY

Why do men earn more?

The gender pay gap can be explained in part by discrimination. Although it's against the law in many countries, women are still paid less than men for the same work. Persistent gender stereotypes are also partly to blame. Women are more likely to be in low-paid jobs associated with "feminine" attributes, such as nursing, while traditionally "male" jobs are better paid. On top of that, men are more likely to have senior roles that command larger pay packets.

Research has shown that women are more likely to take on the majority of childcare responsibilities, despite having a career, too – leading to the so-called "motherhood gap" where women who have children are paid less than women who don't. Sophie Walker, leader of the Women's Equality Party in the UK, argues that the main reason for the pay gap is the high expense of childcare, which may limit the hours women are able to work and cause them to miss

BREAD AND ROSES

In 1912, American activist Elizabeth Gurley Flynn fought for equal pay for women. She was a key organizer in the "Bread and Roses" strike, when textile workers carried signs saying "we want bread and roses too". They were campaigning for better wages, more dignified conditions, and access to education and culture.

out on opportunities due to this. It gets worse if you factor in other inequalities. The American Association of University Women, an advocacy group for equity, reports on the gender gap each year. It includes data on race, age, disability, and sexual identity. This data shows that the pay gap also varies with racial profiles: Hispanic women earn only 54 per cent of what white men are paid. Age also plays a role in widening the gap. The older a female worker is, the less she earns compared to her male counterparts.

Parity, not disparity

Many countries are trying to tackle this problem. Policies encouraging companies to hire and promote women are more widespread, as well as legislation that forces employers to publish pay gap statistics and keep the issue in the spotlight. In Iceland, which in 2017 had the smallest gender gap, childcare is provided by the government – perhaps one of the reasons why Icelandic women have a near-equal participation in the workforce.

See also: 100–103, 114–115

Older women face greater pay discrimination than workers at the start of their careers.

"Unfair pay has prevailed for far too long without consequences."

Serena Williams, US tennis player (2017)

Is LANGUAGE man-made?

His words or hers – what effect does language have on gender equality? Feminists argue that the way we talk about men and women reinforces stereotypes. But is it all talk or can words really devalue women?

MOTIVATED

POWERFUL

DRIVEN

DECISIVE

ANGRY

KNOWLEDGEABLE

DIFFERENT WORDS ARE USED TO DESCRIBE BEHAVIOURS IN MEN...

Is language neutral?

Australian feminist Dale Spender wrote a book on the subject of gender and the English language (*Man Made Language*, 1980) in which she argues that "language is not neutral", but is man-made. The words and phrases we use today were created in a heavily male-focused culture and still reflect sexist attitudes. Have you ever noticed how a mixed gender group can be refered to as "guys" but never as "girls"? Language assumes men to be the norm and women to be the "other". Therefore, we see calling a woman by a male term as fine, but calling a man by a female term as negative – upholding the position of men as superior to women.

Jobs for the girls

This situation has implications for women's position in the workplace. For example, when women take on jobs that were once considered male-only roles, the use of

"Language helps form the limits of our reality."

Dale Spender, *Man Made Language* (1980)

terms such as "female engineer" or the addition of "-ess" (as in "manageress") implies that males are the default option, and that women are a secondary choice or a special exception. Gender neutral terms are increasingly being used, but entrenched bias towards men is still evident.

Words and gender

Certain words also seem to follow women around the workplace. In 2013, US business magazine *Fortune* investigated whether or not men and women are described differently by their bosses by looking at performance reviews from the male-dominated technology industry. It found that while men received constructive criticism asking them to develop certain skills, women received more personal criticism, such as being called "irrational", and being advised to "pay attention to their tone". The word "abrasive" alone cropped up numerous times in the female samples. Other studies have shown similar results: a man can be "confident" while a woman showing the same behaviour is more negatively described using words like "abrasive", "strident", and "bossy".

WOMEN'S WRITING

French feminist writer Hélène Cixous has called on women to write in a different way. In "The Laugh of the Medusa" (1975), she urged women not to try and write like men in order to be accepted into the male-centric status quo, but instead to create a new form of writing based around their unique female qualities and bodies – an "écriture féminine". In 1974, she founded the Centre for Women's Studies at the University of Paris VIII (below, Cixous centre right).

Woman up!

Our language is littered with examples of male-positive ("man up!") and female-negative ("run like a girl") expressions. But many organizations are working to improve the way we talk about women in the workplace. The LeanIn organization, founded to empower businesswomen, started the #BANBOSSY campaign, to discourage the use of this negative word for female leaders. The Women's Media Center suggests the use of a "rule of reversibility" – if you wouldn't say it about a man (for example, words like "shrill" and "feisty"), don't say it about a woman.

AGGRESSIVE

PUSHY

SELFISH

CONTROLLING

MOODY

OPINIONATED

...THAN THOSE USED TO DESCRIBE THE SAME BEHAVIOURS IN WOMEN.

What is MANSPLAINING?

The word "mansplaining" describes how a man explains a subject to a woman in a manner that she finds condescending, assuming that she knows nothing about it; often the explanation is unnecessary. The term is recent, but its meaning is rooted in a history of male domination and silencing of women's voices.

The origins of mansplaining

American feminist writer Rebecca Solnit was falsely credited with coining "mansplaining" after her 2008 essay "Men Explain Things To Me" went viral. Although Solnit had not used the word "mansplain", many women related to the experience she described. A man at a party explained her book (which he had not read) to her, assuming that he knew more about the subject from a review than she, a woman (who happened to be the author), could possibly know. Solnit has described it as "that dynamic in which some men assume they know when they don't, and that the woman they're talking to doesn't when she does." Women took to Twitter, using the hashtag #mansplaining, to

share their experiences and, in 2012, female academics set up "Academic Men Explain Things To Me", a website to share stories of having men explain their own research to them. As Solnit has said, "Mansplaining

> ## "Men explain things to me, and to other women, whether or not they know what they're talking about."
>
> **Rebecca Solnit, "Men Explain Things to Me"**

 See also: 110–111, 114–115

PERHAPS

I THINK...

I KNOW

MAYBE

is not a universal flaw of the gender, just the intersection between overconfidence and cluelessness where some portion of that gender gets stuck." Or, not all men mansplain – only those who are a little bit pleased with themselves and lack self-awareness.

Look who's talking

It can be argued that mansplaining is a way that men unconsciously (or not) keep women in their place – passive and quiet – claiming the expertise to speak for themselves and devaluing women's knowledge. Writing for *The New York Times* in 2017, former Wall Street chief executive and Silicon Valley entrepreneur Sallie Krawcheck described how a male venture capitalist mansplained the difficulty of managing financial advisers to her – despite her high-level experience in business and finance.

"Manterrupting" is another new word used to describe an old practice: how men dominate conversation and silence women's voices. A 1975 study by sociologists Don Zimmerman and Candace West found that in mixed-gender conversations, men made 98 per cent of interruptions. Like mansplaining, manterrupting is a mechanism that prevents women from talking and being heard.

The right to speak

Mansplaining can be seen to show that men are more used to being listened to than women. This indicates that men hold more power, giving them more authority. Undermining women's voices can have grave consequences. In her essay, Solnit writes:

"credibility is a survival tool". Ensuring that women are both heard and heeded is at the heart of the feminist struggle to be taken seriously. For example, in order to have workplace harassment treated as a serious offence, women must first be able to speak and be listened to; only then can their experiences be believed. Inequality will persist until all women have the right to make themselves heard.

WOMEN'S VOICES

Women are often criticized in sexist ways for how they talk – for example, they are said to talk too much despite evidence that men talk more. Young women are judged for speech mannerisms including vocal fry (a low, creaky vibration at the back of the throat) and uptalk (the habit of turning statements into questions). Critics say this makes them sound less competent and authoritative, but policing women's voices – with a preference for more masculine speech traits – is a way of undermining women.

I'LL MAKE IT CLEAR

LET ME EXPLAIN

Women
IN CHARGE

Women all over the world fought for the right to vote in political elections, but how often can they use their votes to put other women in power? Gender inequality is still alive and well in politics: women occupy less than a quarter of the world's parliamentary seats and female heads of state are scarce. The majority of countries have never been led by a woman.

Out of office

Women's voices are too rarely heard in governments worldwide. In 2017, the United Nations presented a snapshot of women in power, and it is not an encouraging picture. There was improvement in Latin America, with more female heads of state being elected, but elsewhere progress has been slow or non-existent. In previous bright spots, such as Africa and Scandinavia, the numbers of women politicians are falling. If the people in power are predominantly male, governments cannot fully represent gender-diverse populations. Women need to be involved in making the laws that affect their lives, so what is keeping them out of office in so many parts of the world?

Bias and ballots

Politics is an expensive and highly competitive business. Women are capable of raising money, mobilizing action, and winning elections, yet some people still do not see politics as a "woman's job". Moreover, while growing numbers are happy to support a well-qualified female candidate, in the gender-biased world of politics not enough women are being recruited. Party recruiters tend to seek candidates in the traditional, male-dominated pools of political talent, such as law firms, rather than reaching out into traditionally more

MINISTER AND MOTHER

The 40th Prime Minister of New Zealand, Jacinda Ardern, had no problem deciding whether to enter politics or be a mother. She did both, giving birth to a daughter in June 2018, just months after election. She is only the second modern government leader, after former Pakistani Prime Minister Benazir Bhutto in 1990, to have a baby while in office.

WOMEN CAN CLIMB TO POWER BUT

female-dominated sectors, such as education and child welfare. However, some political action groups, such as Emily's List in the US, aim to buck the trend by helping to prepare and train women to run for office.

See also: 22–25, 96–97, 110–111, 128–129

Just 23 per cent of the world's parliamentary politicians are female.

A question of confidence?

Another problem is that too few women want to run for office at all. This has often been put down to a lack of confidence, as high-achieving women have been shown to consider themselves more unqualified for office than men. However, it may also be the case that women do not receive the support and validation for their ambitions that men do. Studies in the US have shown that men in college are much more likely to be encouraged to run for office than women are, leading to a gap in male and female political ambitions. Women may also be put off by the campaigning involved, as they might expect greater scrutiny and criticism because of their gender.

Run and run

One way to bring more women into office is to use gender quotas, which lay down the minimum number of women that must appear on a list of candidates for election. Around 45 countries use these. There is also strong evidence that every woman in office inspires others to enter politics. A study of the 2015 election campaign in Israel found that female candidates generated higher engagement using social media than men. Looking at politicians in more than 100 countries, the National Democratic Institute for International Affairs also found that women tend to be more responsive to constituents and more likely to focus on issues important to other women, such as health and education.

> **"What is democracy? Is it people for the people or men for the people?"**
>
> **Phumzile Mlambo-Ngcuka, Executive Director of UN Women (2017)**

GENDER BIAS MAY STOP THEM REACHING THE VERY TOP

CULTURE and SOCIETY

The BEAUTY myth

Do FEMINISTS wear HEELS?

BODY image

The MALE GAZE

Does SEX sell?

Women in the MEDIA

Social MEDIA

Becoming INVISIBLE

Is PORNOGRAPHY ever OKAY?

Feminism and SEX WORK

WOMEN of the world UNITE!

A global FEMINISM

Can MEN be FEMINISTS?

The society we live in shapes how we view ourselves and others. Advertising, social media, and popular culture all play a part. Feminists have looked at the representation of women in the media and questioned what it says about how society views women. They have pushed for more diverse representation and a more global feminist outlook.

The **BEAUTY** myth

Feminists believe that the beauty industry creates anxiety for women around their appearance by projecting particular images of beauty. Women feel pressured to live up to these ideals and can suffer from low self-esteem if they feel they fall short. The beauty industry profits by selling the idea that if you buy their products you will look thinner, younger, and more beautiful.

A woman's worth

US journalist and feminist Naomi Wolf, in her book *The Beauty Myth* (1990), says that it is not natural or innate for women to want to be beautiful and for men to value beauty above all else. Rather, the culture we live in imposes narrow beauty standards, which work to sustain social, political, and economic control over women. According to Wolf, before the 1960s, women's social value was largely dependent on domesticity, but now the beauty myth has become the dominant form of social value. Feminists believe that the association between beauty and femininity works to oppress women. Within the beauty myth, women's bodies have become the prison the home once was.

Who defines beauty?

Beauty ideals have varied through history and across different cultures, but today in the West these are to be young, thin, white, and able-bodied; those who do not fit these ideals are devalued. A huge number of the images we see in the media are airbrushed and retouched, giving a false impression of how even models look. This is common not only on the pages of glossy

DO WOMEN FEEL PRESSURE TO LIVE UP TO SOCIETY'S IDEA OF BEAUTY?

magazines, but also on social media platforms such as Instagram, where people can apply filters to make themselves look more attractive. In this way, social media is extremely powerful when it comes to reinforcing ideas about "beauty" and "perfect bodies". This can be damaging to the confidence of young girls, who are not only comparing themselves to models and actresses, but also to their peers.

Is beauty controlling?

The beauty myth is also about behaviour. For example, the removal of female body hair is considered desirable in Western cultures, while for feminists it represents another means of controlling women. Today, sporting body hair is often interpreted as "making a statement", as demonstrated by the sensationalist and negative reactions when Hollywood actor Julia Roberts appeared with underarm hair on the red carpet in 1999. Women with hair anywhere but their heads are labelled as "unkempt", "messy", or "gross", and so they feel pressured to conform to traditional standards of beauty.

For Wolf, the cultural obsession with female appearance is about controlling women. Trying to live up to beauty ideals can be exhausting, time-consuming, and expensive. When women are preoccupied with how they look they may not be fulfilling their potential in other ways. Wolf uses the phrase "cultural conspiracy": women who feel ugly or old will buy beauty products they don't really need, and still feel inferior or inadequate since living up to beauty ideals is an impossible goal. Wolf observed that the more liberated women have become, the more the pressure to conform to rigid beauty ideals has increased.

Being beautiful

Wolf said that the real problem was lack of choice. Girls and women may wear make-up or shave their legs to express their femininity, but they should not be confined to harmful ideals of beauty that say the only way to be beautiful is to be thin, light skinned, and able-

bodied. There are more and more examples of women and girls speaking out against the imposition of beauty ideals, and in reaction to women's voices and buying power some clothing brands have decided to not retouch images of their models.
However, there's a long way to go. Dismantling traditional beauty standards does not mean women have to put down the razor and stop wearing make-up. Feminists argue we need to redefine beauty, and that can still be done wearing the brightest red lipstick.

SELLING FEMINISM

In her 2016 book, *We Were Feminists Once*, American feminist Andi Zeisler suggests that modern feminism has been co-opted by the marketplace to sell beauty products. She explores how marketing campaigns aimed at empowering women or improving self-esteem are being used to sell products that still ultimately play on women's anxiety about their appearance.

The global cosmetics industry is thought to be worth in the region of $500 billion dollars.

See also: 52–53, 120–127, 130–133

> ## "She wins who calls herself beautiful and challenges the world to change to truly see her."
>
> Naomi Wolf, *The Beauty Myth* (1990)

Do FEMINISTS wear HEELS?

High heels go in and out of fashion, and for many feminists they're just a part of their individual style. To other feminists, however, they are a symbol of oppression – heels inflict pain, restrict movement, and reinforce negative feminine stereotypes. So who's right?

Femininity

High-heeled shoes are designed to make the wearer look more "feminine" – the arched heel highlighting the leg length and the shapely curves of the lower body. Media and the fashion industry commonly portray women wearing high heels, helping to create an idealized woman who looks sexy, happy, and successful. Some feminists argue that this objectifies women, and sets unrealistic beauty standards for them to live up to.

Self-expression

Other feminists argue that fashion is not oppressive, but that what you wear can be an enjoyable form of self-expression, identity, and empowerment. British feminist fashion theorist Joanne Entwistle argues that some women take pleasure in their fashion choices and use them to create their own identities. Some women say that they wear heels because it makes them feel strong and dominant. American fashion historian Valerie Steele believes heels can express a woman's power, placing a dangerous weapon – the stiletto (a tapered blade for stabbing) – within arm's reach.

The association of high heels with power is long-standing. In fact, heeled shoes were invented in the 10th century, for the Persian cavalry, to keep the boots of male riders in their stirrups. Owning a horse was a status

HIGH HEELS CAN BE SEEN AS A SYMBOL OF OPPRESSION OR POWER

symbol, so anyone in heeled boots was someone important. Later, men in 16th-century Europe wore high heels as a symbol of prestige, to set themselves above (literally) the rest of society. It is perhaps a combination of the historical association with status, the design of the shoes, plus the extra height they give, that help to make women feel powerful in a male-dominated world.

A painful matter

High heels became a hot topic after a series of media stories sparked a debate over whether wearing heels oppresses women by causing them discomfort and injury. Heels are certainly not designed for walking far, or at speed, yet some dress codes still require women to wear them. In 2016, a temporary receptionist sent to work at accountancy firm PwC in London, UK, was sent home without pay for refusing to wear high heels. Nicola Thorp argued that wearing smart flats did not affect her ability to do her work (and that nine hours on her feet in heels would have been impossibly uncomfortable) and pointed out male colleagues had not been asked to do the same. She launched a petition calling for a new law restricting workplace dress codes, which was debated in parliament.

UNEQUAL DRESS CODES

In 2015, women were outraged when a security guard at Cannes Film Festival refused to admit several female film stars wearing flats because a dress code requires them to wear heels. A few actors have since protested against this. In 2018, American star Kirsten Stewart went barefoot on the red carpet to make her point that insisting women wear heels is discrimination.

See also: 118–119, 128–129

Freedom to choose?

In the end, it's all about the freedom of choice and self-expression. Feminists do wear high heels and they also wear flat shoes. Women should be able to choose and not have a certain style imposed upon them.

A 17th-century painting of King Louis XIV of France shows him in very high red heels.

BODY image

What is the "ideal" shape for a woman's body? At the moment, in the West, thin is in; skinny (usually young, white, and able-bodied) celebrities dominate the Internet, TV, and magazines. Images of this "perfect" body shape set an impossible standard for women and girls to live up to and lead to many women feeling dissatisfied and unhappy with their bodies.

How do I look?

How women look is given such importance in modern society that it can affect their health and self-esteem. In 1978, British psychotherapist Susie Orbach wrote *Fat is a Feminist Issue*, which proposed that women overeat as a reaction to society's pressures to be the "perfect" woman. Orbach believes that women strive to be thin to conform to their ideas of attractiveness and success, but

COMPARING THEMSELVES WITH IMPOSSIBLE

MEASURING UP

This advertisement for a diet drink showing an idealized "beach body" was banned from London Underground after 70,000 people signed an online petition. London's mayor Sadiq Khan said he was concerned about advertising that makes women ashamed of their bodies.

for some being fat is an unconscious way to avoid competing and rebuff sexual advances. For many women, however, the pressure to look slim sets up a vicious circle of dieting and comfort eating. Millions of women spend much of their lives on a diet, trying to achieve the "ideal" look, even though evidence shows

"I don't think I am ugly, but I hate how the world responds to this body."

Roxane Gay, *Hunger* (2017)

diets don't work. The diet and fitness industries know this and cash in on women's insecurities about their bodies, while advertising and the media perpetuate women's unhappiness with their image (see pp.118–121). In *Unbearable Weight* (2003), American academic Susan Bordo suggests that dieting is considered so normal in our culture that healthy teenagers try to emulate the impossible images they see by controlling their bodies with excessive dieting. This desire to be thin affects younger and younger children. A study by Common Sense Media (2015) in the US showed that 1 in 4 children had dieted by the age of seven. In extreme cases, dieting leads to obsessive thoughts about food, feelings of shame and guilt, and even depression. It increases the risk of developing an eating disorder such as anorexia nervosa or bulimia, and mental health issues such as self-harm.

See also: 118–121, 124–131

Body positivity

Despite this diet culture, diverse bodies are being increasingly celebrated. Girls are being inspired by strong women in sport, including Paralympians; "plus-size" models such as Ashley Graham; and social media influencers using the hashtag #bodypositivism. Even Barbie now comes in four different body types. However, women such as US writer Roxane Gay have written about the judgements their bodies have faced and how attitudes still need to improve.

IDEALS CAN DISTORT THE WAY GIRLS SEE THEMSELVES

The MALE GAZE

Cultural critics and feminists argue that the way women have been portrayed in art and film reduces them to passive objects for men to enjoy looking at. The idea that art is produced with an imagined male viewer in mind is known as the "male gaze". Feminists are challenging this viewpoint, and creating powerful, active representations of women.

WHAT ARE YOU LOOKING AT?

Painting the female form

In his 1972 book *Ways Of Seeing*, British art critic John Berger wrote that in images where women are portrayed in a different way from men, it is not because the feminine is inherently different from the masculine, but "because the 'ideal' spectator is always assumed to be a man and the image of the woman he looks at is designed to flatter him".

Looking in particular at Renaissance oil paintings of "the nude", Berger noted how paintings of naked women, unlike those of men, are positioned looking outward and their bodies are displayed for an imagined male spectator, who spies on them often as they bathe or sleep. If the male viewpoint is active (looking) while the female is passive (being looked at), the result is that the woman becomes an idealized object of desire, while the man is in a position of power.

See also: 38–39, 86–87, 128–129, 130–131

FEMINISTS ARE CHALLENGING PASSIVE DEPICTIONS OF WOMEN IN ART AND FILM

The male gaze

British feminist film theorist Laura Mulvey called this idea the "male gaze". In 1975, she wrote a book called *Visual Pleasure and Narrative Cinema*, in which she argued that women in Hollywood films have traditionally been objects of desire for both the characters in the film and the audience watching. She examined the way that camera shots tended to zoom in and linger over parts of a woman's body, while men on screen were presented as the active figures driving the story. Since Mulvey coined the term, it has been widely used to refer to the objectification of women in popular culture.

Other feminists pointed out that Mulvey's stance was entirely focused on white women. African American academic bell hooks questioned how black women are supposed to relate to cinema when the cinematic gaze is not just male but white. Queer theorists, including Patricia White in the US, have examined what the male gaze means for lesbians when the intended viewer is assumed to be a heterosexual male.

Looking forward

Women are increasingly resisting the male gaze by exposing it and creating their own images on their own terms. In film, this is happening, but slowly. Recent statistics from the "celluloid ceiling report" by San Diego University in the US show that the number of women directors of the top grossing US films is slowly climbing but still sits at only 11 per cent.

In the art world, too, female representation has been challenged. Women artists, such as Frida Kahlo (Mexico), Marlene Dumas (South Africa), Paula Rego (Portugal), and Jenny Saville (UK), have tried to find new ways of representing women's bodies, exploring the naked truth, rather than idealizing women for the male gaze.

THE FEMALE GAZE

The 17th-century Italian painter Artemisia Gentileschi was one of the most progressive and celebrated painters of the Renaissance, when art was primarily a male pursuit. She is renowned for her depictions of strong, sensual women, such as this self-portrait. With her sleeves rolled up to reveal her powerful arms as she paints, the treatment is very different to the passive, objectified depictions of women at the time.

Another way to counteract the male gaze is to get more works by women into exhibitions and galleries – to promote the female gaze. In 1985, feminist activist group the Guerilla Girls mounted a protest against the exclusion of women from the New York Museum of Modern Art in the US and the art world generally. One poster read, "Do women have to be naked to get into the Met. Museum? Less than five percent of the artists in the Modern Art sections are women, but 85 per cent of the nudes are female". In 2011, they did a recount and found that four per cent of the artists in the Modern and Contemporary sections were women, but 76 per cent of the nudes were female.

> ## "The image of women as we know it is an image created by men and fashioned to suit their needs."
>
> ### Kate Millett *Sexual Politics* (1970)

Does SEX sell?

The advertising industry needs women. Women are its largest audience, wielding around 80 per cent of consumer spending power, due to their influence on the buying decisions of boyfriends, husbands, and children. Yet advertisers have taken a long time to start casting women that other women can relate to.

Selling stereotypes

Since the 1960s, feminists have protested against the way in which advertisements show women in particular roles – typically as wives, mothers, and homemakers. Such gender stereotyping reinforces narrow ideas about gender roles and can restrict the aspirations of young people, according to a US study by Harvard University in 2011. For example, when adverts repeatedly show a woman doing all the cooking and cleaning in a family, it adds force to the idea that domestic activities are a woman's responsibility. Women have been, and continue to be portrayed as sexual objects in advertising. In fact, 96 per cent of objectifying images in advertising are of women, according to American feminist Caroline Heldman. It is easy to dismiss adverts as no big deal, but research shows that the way people are portrayed in advertising has the potential to affect self-esteem. A 2011 study led by Debra Trampe in the Netherlands indicated that looking at airbrushed images of models in

> **"The way in which men and women are portrayed in advertising becomes internalized by individuals as social norms."**
>
> **Jacqui Hunt, director of Equality Now (2018)**

advertisements makes women feel dissatisfied with their own appearance. Gender stereotyping can also have a negative impact on men, when they feel they are expected to live up to the typical advertising view of them as sporty, macho, and confident. A 2012

European Parliament report emphasized the importance of eliminating gender stereotypes from advertising because it reinforces assumptions about men and women and distorts how people see themselves.

What's changed?

Over the last decade, female consumers have become more critical of adverts that feature sexist stereotypes. However, joint research by the Geena Davis Institute and ad agency J. Walter Thompson in 2017, found that the representation of women in advertising has not improved – in fact, women are getting younger and "dumber", they say. In their study men were 89 per cent more likely than women to be shown as intelligent (up from 62 per cent the year before), men were on screen four times as often as women, and spoke seven times as much. Women in adverts are mostly in their 20s compared to men who are represented at greater range of ages. And one in 10 female

AD BAN

Sexist adverts are seen on billboards in cities around the world. In 2018, authorities in Stockholm, Sweden, voted to ban sexist advertising from public spaces. The Swedish advertising authorities have been granted the right to remove offending adverts that depict men or women as sex objects, or in a way that shows stereotypical gender roles, from any of the 700 city-owned billboards.

ICH RESERVIE**HRS.**

characters are shown in sexually revealing clothing, six times more than male characters. However, there is a demand for change. A global survey by Unilever, which makes some of the world's best known cosmetic brands, indicated that 40 per cent of women could not relate to the women in adverts. Another international study by Cambridge University, UK, found that female consumers preferred brands that used models who mirrored their own identities and represented real women.

Femvertising

In response to the growing demand for more realistic and diverse images of beauty, some advertisers have begun to change the types of women featured in their adverts. The US brand Billie has received huge praise for being the first company in decades to feature women with body hair in their adverts. The "Like A Girl" ad by feminine hygiene brand Always made fun of the idea that girls supposedly can't do things as well as men, and various sportswear makers, such as Nike and Under Armour, have made commercials that show strong women overcoming adversity. However, this growing trend for empowered women in advertising has been dubbed "Femvertising", and some feminists have accused advertisers of hijacking feminist ideas in order to sell products, while doing nothing to tackle gender inequality in their own companies.

Women in the MEDIA

Since the media is powerful enough to influence the public's views, what happens when it is run and presented mostly by men? Although women represent half the audience for television, radio, newspapers, and magazines, most media bosses are men and men hold a far greater number of senior positions.

Women in the limelight

Feminists argue that since the media is dominated by men, then it is almost impossible for women to be equally represented, free from stereotypes. Men occupy 73 per cent of top management positions in the media globally, according to a 2011 study by the International Women's Media Foundation. The Global Media Monitoring Project researched news coverage across 114 countries in 2015, and found that in TV, newspaper, and radio news women accounted for just 24 per cent of the people seen, heard, or written about.

When women do make it into the media they are judged more by how they look than by what they have to say. In films and TV shows women are more likely to be portrayed as passive, submissive, or as victims. For example, in 2014, international research by The Geena Davis Institute on gender images in films found that less than one-third of all speaking characters were female. Less than a quarter of the fictional workforce were women and when women were employed, they were largely absent from powerful positions. Women were also twice as likely as men to be naked or in revealing clothing. The media is a trusted source of information and therefore its representation of women can reinforce ideas about gender roles and deepen negative stereotypes.

See also: 114–115, 118–119

Undermining power

Women are rarely presented as being powerful or influential in the media. Even when women in power make the news, the headlines focus on their appearance or fashion choices. What they have to say is secondary, which devalues the political voices of women as a whole. For example, the socialist government elected in Spain in 2018 has the most female-dominated cabinet in Europe. But their

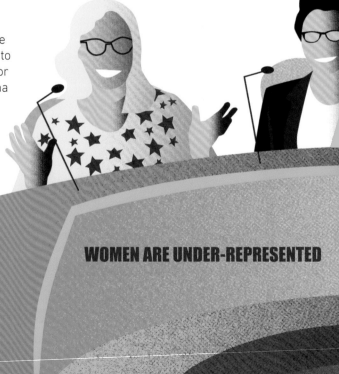

WOMEN ARE UNDER-REPRESENTED

> ## "If I want to knock a story off the front page, I just change my hairstyle."
>
> **Hillary Clinton, UN Women's Conference in Beijing (1995)**

gal-dem

UK online magazine *gal-dem* is one of the publications changing the face of the media. It was launched in 2015 by Liv Little who felt frustrated by the lack of diversity among women in the media, and wanted to provide a space for non-white women to share their experiences.

the gal-hood issue

power has been undermined by the Spanish newspaper ABC, which only acknowledged the new female ministers on its fashion pages – of course the men in the cabinet were missed out. The paper wrote that the health minister, Carmen Montón Giménez, "has a good body that she should make more of", while industry minister Reyes Maroto was criticized for wearing "skirts too short for someone in her post". Two US studies by the "Name It, Change It" project show that when the media comments on the appearance of female politicians or uses sexist rhetoric, it negatively impacts on how voters view them. They might be seen as less trustworthy or qualified.

As well as being subjected to scrutiny around their appearance, women are under-represented as experts, too. When journalists reporting for television, radio, or newspapers turn to an expert, they tend to look to a man. Attempting to change the male bias in the UK press is feminist activist Caroline Criado-Perez. She co-founded "The Women's Room", a website that promotes female experts, in an attempt to get them into the media and have more women's voices heard.

Time for change

Representation is important because it is empowering for women to see people in the media that they can relate to. A lot of feminist magazines grow from the fact that women feel they are under-represented in the media, or that the issues that affect them are not being spoken about. Feminist magazines *BBY* in Sweden, *Sukeban* ("boss girl") in Japan, and *Femini* in the UK are devoted to inspiring diversity and discussing the struggles and successes of women around the world. There have been signs of change in the mainstream media, too. For example *Teen Vogue* magazine in the US introduced a fashion section for plus-size women and lobbied for the Senate to approve the Equal Rights Amendment.

IN ALL AREAS OF MEDIA COVERAGE

Social MEDIA

The amount of time people spend on social media is increasing globally. Social media connects people, it gives voice to less powerful groups in society, and it can provide a tool for activism. But young women are facing immense pressure because a lot of what they see online sets impossible standards for how they should look, or how they should live.

See also: 66–67, 118–119

Social media vs reality

Social media has become integral to all our lives. Research by the UK Education Policy Institute (EPI) in 2017 found that more than one in three British 15-year-olds spend at least six hours a day online – which is more than their counterparts in the other countries studied, apart from Chile. Social media platforms such as Twitter, Facebook, and Instagram are places where people share their experiences with social networks. Research has found that this can be a positive experience and allows people to connect with others who share similar interests. For example, sociologists Katherine Larson and Lynne Zubernis have studied "fandoms" (fans of books or TV shows) in the US, who use social media to create communities and produce creative work of their own. However, the EPI research reported a correlation between hours spent on social media and negative effects on wellbeing. A lot of people share only the high points in their lives, or flattering images of themselves. On social media, a person's worth is measured by the number of followers they have or the number of "likes" a post receives, which can cause anxiety or low self-esteem. English feminist Laura Bates, in her book *Girl Up* (2016), renamed social media platforms "Fitter", "Fakebook", and "Instaglam" to remind us that a lot of what appears online does not reflect reality.

Clicktivism

Lots of people use social media for activism, too. It connects people, builds communities, and provides a space where marginalized people can be themselves.

Before, if women wanted to team up to protest against discrimination, they relied on rallies, written petitions, and letters. The rise of social media has made it easier for women to voice their opinions because online spaces are easily accessed and everyone is equally entitled to speak out, unlike other forms of media that are controlled by powerful people.

Social media has also enabled a new wave of "clicktivists" who use social media as their weapon in the fight for equality. An early example of this came in 2012, when a schoolgirl from the US state of Maine, Julia Bluhm, launched an appeal on petition website

INSTA-TRICKS

Instagram is full of images of fitness bloggers with perfect bodies, but pictures can be deceptive. The Finnish blogger Sara Puhto posted photos to highlight how different angles and lighting can drastically alter how fit and toned her body looks. Similarly, Australian bikini designer Karina Irby posted images that highlight the difference retouching makes.

> ## "Social media is something of a double-edged sword."
> **Roxane Gay (2013)**

change.org that convinced *Seventeen* magazine to stop altering images of models. There are now numerous examples of hashtag activism among women who have used social media platforms to raise awareness, gather support, and force companies and governments to change the way they treat women. In India, a 2013 hashtag campaign helped persuade the Indian government to introduce stricter rape laws. In Afghanistan, women used social media in 2017 to shame a high-ranking army officer who was demanding sexual favours from female colleagues, and he was fired as a result.

Online abuse

Unfortunately, some women that have started online campaigns have experienced a backlash. Internet trolls attempt to silence women through abusive language. For example, French journalist Anaïs Condomines received death and rape threats after writing a news story about an anti-feminist video-gaming forum. However, trolls don't necessarily win. Criola, a Brazilian civil rights advocacy group run by women, began their "Virtual Racism, Real Consequences" campaign in 2015, when Afro-Brazilian meteorologist, Maria Júlia Coutinho, became the target of extreme online abuse. Criola published the racist posts on billboards around Brazilian cities. As a result, most of the commenters deleted their social media accounts.

ONLINE IMAGES MAY NOT REFLECT REALITY

LOOKING GORGEOUS!

HEY, BEAUTIFUL.

YOUR DRESS LOOKS AMAZING.

YOU COULD SERIOUSLY BE A MODEL

I WISH I COULD LIKE THIS TWICE.

HOW DO YOU ALWAYS LOOK SO GOOD?

STOP BEING SO BEAUTIFUL!

Becoming
INVISIBLE

In Western societies, a high value is placed on how a woman looks. The ideals of beauty that flood advertisements, magazines, and film and television screens are usually thin, white, able-bodied, and, above all, young. Feminists are concerned with how negative stereotypes and under-representation in the media devalue older women and keep inequalities in place.

See also: 118–119, 128–129

Is age just a number?

Ageing not only brings physical changes such as greying hair, but also a change in how a person is perceived by society. In many countries, both sexes experience ageism (discrimination because of their age), but older women are more subject to negative stereotyping than older men. Media researcher Dafna Lemish and psychologist Varda Muhlbauer's work "Can't Have it All" (2012) suggests that older women become invisible or are stereotyped as "the controlling mother, the plain, uneducated, but good housewife, and the bitch-witch older woman." The authors argue that after the menopause, when women lose their fertility – one of the measures of femininity – they lose their primary social value as child-bearers. They are also presumed to have lost their sexuality, further diminishing their feminine identity. A man, on the other hand, may retain his social value into old age, regardless of health and fitness, because of his perceived knowledge and accumulated life experience.

AS WOMEN LEAVE THEIR YOUTH BEHIND, DO THEY FADE AWAY IN THE PUBLIC

> ## "I refuse to let a system, a culture... tell me I don't matter."
>
> **Oprah Winfrey, media star (2014, aged 60)**

Vanishing from the screen

One of the most obvious areas in which older women are under-represented is popular culture. As Lemish and Muhlbauer found, when women mature, they vanish from the screen. In comparison to older men, women appear in about one-third of roles for older adults and roles for strong women are rare.

In romantic films, older women are not usually portrayed as being desirable or the love interest, whereas older male characters often have on-screen romances with younger women. In one instance, the actor Maggie Gyllenhaal was considered too old at only 37 years of age to play the love interest of a 55-year-old man. The older women who do appear in films and TV shows are often praised for their youthful looks. British academic Deborah Jermyn's work highlights how even when directors, such as Nancy Meyers, put older

AGEISM AND SEXISM

In 2011, Irish television presenter Miriam O'Reilly won a landmark age discrimination case against the BBC. A tribunal found the broadcasting company guilty of ageism after O'Reilly was dropped from her countryside affairs show at the age of 53. The tribunal rejected her additional claim of sexism and O'Reilly chose not to pursue the matter.

women into leading roles they are dismissed by critics as catering only to an older female audience. Since screen life can be seen to mirror real life, such portrayals can impact on how women experience ageing and undermine their self-esteem and their sense of desirability – as well as suggesting that life is not rewarding after a certain age.

Positive ageing

Feminists say that ageing can be a resistance, as women refuse to be invisible. And mature women with valuable life experience often make good role models for younger women. A posse of women over 60 have taken to Instagram to show by their clothes and lifestyles that they're still – in the words of 64-year-old Professor Lyn Slater – "really freaking cool". By showing ageing that does not conform to the negative stereotypes portrayed in media, these images are encouraging a change in public perception. As sociologist Laura C. Hurd suggests in "We're not Old": "being old does not necessarily and inevitably mean that one is senile, tired, sickly, and frail".

IMAGINATION?

Is PORNOGRAPHY ever OKAY?

There is no other issue that divides feminists as much as pornography. Some have criticized it for its unrealistic portrayal of intimate relationships, which can give young people inaccurate ideas about sex, while others suggest watching sex-positive porn can be healthy.

Porn in the Internet age

Pornography is any sexually explicit image or video that is designed to titillate or arouse its viewer. It ranges from "soft-core" porn that may show partial nudity to "hard-core" porn that displays more extreme acts. In the Internet age pornography has become much easier to find, much of it is free, and it can sometimes be found accidentally while browsing the Internet.

See also: 88–89, 138–139

THE INVENTION OF THE INTERNET HAS LED TO EASIER ACCESS TO PORNOGRAPHY

Anti-porn

Much pornography is aimed at men and features women being dominated by men. As a result, some feminists, such as American lawyer Catharine MacKinnon, argue that pornography oppresses women and gives those who watch it unrealistic ideas about sex – that women enjoy violence and being powerless during sex, and men can do what they like to women. In 2010, US psychologist Ana Bridges and her colleagues found that 82 per cent of 304 popular pornographic scenes displayed at least one physically aggressive act. They observed that the targets of the aggression (mostly women) "often showed pleasure or responded neutrally to the aggression." In 2015, UNESCO reported that after watching porn men feel less empathy and more aggression towards women.

American anti-pornography activist Andrea Dworkin's controversial book *Pornography: Men Possessing Women* (1981) argued that pornography celebrated rape and injury to women. Her ideas sparked debate amongst feminists, some of whom argued that actors in pornography are doing it because they want to.

Sex-positive feminists

In the 1990s and 2000s, some feminists began to rethink criticism against pornography. Many were not anti-pornography in itself, but against the unrealistic portrayal of sex that it often gave and that it was mostly aimed at men. They suggested there is nothing wrong with pornography so long as it is sex-positive and made with women's (as well as men's) interests in mind. British academics Clarissa Smith and Feona Attwood found that people, including women, used porn to explore their sexuality and argued that there is nothing shameful about this. If a woman enjoys watching certain types of pornography, and the actors in it are being paid fairly and treated equally, then perhaps there is no harm in it.

Porn and young people

Some feminists have expressed concern that young people are learning about sex from porn and that it may lead them to develop unrealistic expectations for sex and relationships. However, others have questioned whether porn consumption is always negative or if it can lead to positive discussion.

PUBLIC HEALTH Some schools in Denmark have introduced discussion of pornography into their sex-education curriculum, so they can educate young people about real intimate relationships versus those shown in pornography. Danish sexologist Christian Graugaard argues this is not enough and that it should be introduced in school curriculums across the country, so all young people can be educated about real sex and relationships.

British activist-academic Meg-John Barker and sex educator Justin Hancock argue that the harmful effects of porn have been overstated. They suggest that young people who consume porn are affected in more complex ways than anti-porn arguments suggest, and are capable of critiquing it using their pre-existing ideas about sex and relationships. Barker and Hancock suggest that what is needed is more extensive and inclusive material and education for young people around relationships and sex, as existing sex education is "too little, too late and too biological". Teaching young people on a wider range of topics will better prepare them for relationships – both those who watch porn and those who do not.

> **"74 per cent of 11–18 year olds said that porn should be discussed in sex education."**
>
> NSPCC, UK sex education survey (2013)

Alice Schwarzer

Born 1942

Germany's most famous feminist, journalist, and publisher, Alice Schwarzer became a force in the women's movement of the 1970s and 1980s, campaigning for legal abortion and against sexual violence. Schwarzer became expert at using the media to get her often controversial message across, and started *EMMA*, Europe's longest-running feminist magazine. She has written more than 20 books.

> **"Don't seek to be loved at any price! Be open to conflict!"**

A voice for women

Born during World War II, Alice Schwarzer was raised by her grandparents, who helped to shape her outlook. Her grandmother was a political activist, while her grandfather took care of the household. After training as a journalist Schwarzer worked in France, where she got involved in the 1960s women's movement. She took the fight for equality to Germany, at the time a traditional society where men had the legal right to stop their wives from working. In 1975, Schwarzer wrote *The Little Difference and its Huge Consequences*, which analysed love and sex as a power game between men and women. She described how many women blamed themselves for issues they had with their partners, while these were caused by the men trying to control women.

Controversial views

In 1971, Schwarzer lobbied for abortion to be made legal in Germany. In the 1980s, she began a campaign against pornography. More recently, she has criticized what she sees as Muslim women's oppression, views some think are feeding Islamophobia.

German media icon

As a columnist for Germany's biggest newspaper, *Das Bild*, Alice Schwarzer has been able to reach a wide audience with her articles on women's rights. In 1977, she launched the German feminist journal *EMMA*, short for emancipation. She also started a publishing house devoted to feminist works, including her own.

Making headlines
Unlike most women's magazines, *EMMA* is not glamorous, focusing purely on political and feminist issues. It is still the only political magazine in Europe run by women.

Outspoken journalist
Alice Schwarzer has written many strongly opinionated articles on topics such as pornography, abortion, prostitution, and whether the hijab should be banned in Germany.

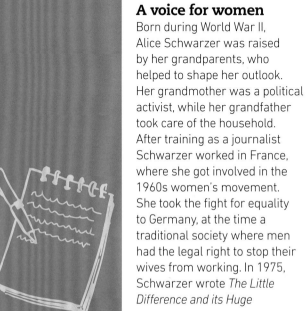

Feminism and
SEX WORK

Sex work is an issue that has strongly divided feminists. Some argue that women should be free to choose their job, whatever it may be, but others argue that sex work exploits women and has no place in today's society.

Working girls

The phrase sex work is often used to refer to prostitution (exchanging sex for money), but it can also encompass other acts such as phone sex, stripping, and erotic dancing. Most sex work is done by women, but there are male sex workers, who usually work for male clients. Feminist arguments surrounding sex work normally focus on men paying women for sex. This can take place on the streets or behind closed doors and has been criminalized in different ways for centuries. As a result, it is difficult for sex workers to report abuse and rape, as they may be treated as criminals and told to expect such ill treatment as part of their work. The Internet has made sex work safer for some, allowing workers to screen potential clients, but for many women around the world it remains dangerous work.

Is sex work exploitative?

Many feminists believe sex work exploits women. US lawyer and activist Catharine MacKinnon is one of several prominent feminists who argue that selling sex is a form of objectification, as it treats women's bodies as sexual commodities, or "objects". MacKinnon and others say sex work is often forced on vulnerable women with no alternatives, and have raised concerns about the violence women experience on the job, as well as the effects it can have on their mental health.

While some feminists favour banning sex work, others argue that making it illegal forces women undercover and into working on the streets, where they are more likely to suffer abuse and become dependent on drugs and alcohol. They say that rather than punishing women, society should instead focus on the men who pay for sex. Some countries such as Sweden have taken this approach and made it illegal to buy sex, but not to sell it. But other countries, among them Germany, Ecuador, and Austria, have fully legalized sex work, and several human rights charities, such as Amnesty International, have also recently come out in support of decriminalization. Governments around the world are still divided on the best approach.

A woman's choice

Many feminists support a full legalization of sex work, in order to guarantee greater safety for those involved. Some of these, such as US theorist Gayle Rubin, have suggested that sex work should be seen as a positive, empowering choice for some women, rather than an act of desperation. Many sex workers themselves, such as US activist Carol Leigh, have also sought to gain rights and respect for sex workers, arguing that women should be able to use their bodies any way they want. These "sex-positive" feminists see criticisms of sex work as based on moralising and sexist ideas that see women's sexual agency as wrong.

LEGALIZATION

Sex work became legal in Germany in 2002 – the new law aimed to give workers rights, contracts, sick pay, and less stigma. However, its success is debated. Since then, only one per cent of workers have signed a legal contract and sex trafficking is thought to have increased. A further law in 2017 aimed to improve regulation, but some sex workers protested against this.

Global problems

Something feminists can agree on is that efforts need to be made to help the many girls and women who are trafficked into the global sex trade. Sex trafficking happens in many countries, but often vulnerable girls are taken from poorer countries to richer ones where they are forced into sex work in exchange for such basics as food and shelter. The International Labour Organization estimates that 4.8 million people live in a state of forced sexual exploitation. Charities are working to end this, but there is still lots to be done.

> "Sex workers are one of the most marginalized groups in the world..."
>
> Salil Shetty, Secretary General of Amnesty International (2015)

EXCHANGING MONEY FOR SEX IS ILLEGAL IN MANY COUNTRIES

Women of the world UNITE!

Since the early days of the women's movement, women have gathered together in non-violent demonstrations – marching for their own liberation and a more peaceful world for all.

Stepping out for peace

There has often been a crossover between feminism and campaigns against militarism, war, and violence. In 1915, building on suffragist activism, pacifist Jane Addams and other American feminists formed the Woman's Peace Party to resist US involvement in World War I. They planned anti-war initiatives such as the 1915 Women's Peace Congress at the Hague, in the Netherlands, where 1,200 women from 12 countries discussed ways to end the war. Addams won the Nobel Peace Prize in 1931. American women also played an important role in the anti-Vietnam War movement of the 1960s and 1970s, demonstrating against the US role in the conflict. In 1968, thousands marched on Washington, DC, led by Women's Strike for Peace (WSP) – an association of women founded by activists Bella Abzug and Dagmar Wilson – to demand a voice in national affairs. A more extreme group called New York Radical Women staged a "Burial of Traditional Womanhood", resisting the passive role of "tearful widows" and uniting as a force to be reckoned with.

In 1961, WSP led 50,000 "concerned housewives" in a march against nuclear testing. In the UK, the Greenham Common Women's Peace Camp

NO TO WAR, VIOLENCE, AND OPPRESSION!

in the 1980s was a women-only protest against nuclear weapons. Women camped at the military base in southeast England to oppose the location of US cruise missiles there, chaining themselves to the fence in protest. At one point, 30,000 women linked arms to "embrace the base" and obstruct weapons delivery. Many were mothers, who left their husbands and children at home to fight for future generations.

> ## "Without community, there is no liberation."
>
> **Audre Lorde, *Sister Outsider* (1984)**

MOTHERS OF THE PLAZA DE MAYO

On 30 April 1977, fourteen mothers gathered in Buenos Aires' main square to confront the dictatorship that had stolen their children. This was the first march by the mothers of Argentina's "disappeared" – 22,000 young people who had been murdered by the regime. Four decades and more than 2,000 marches on, the mothers are still marching.

Taking a stand

In the 21st century, women around the world have united to seek liberation from violence. In the US, three radical black women, Alicia Garza, Opal Tometi, and Patrisse Cullors, formed #BlackLivesMatter in 2013.

This was a call to action after a white vigilante accused of murdering 17-year-old black high-school student Trayvon Martin was acquitted. This black-centred political movement gives a prominent role to women, queer, and trans leaders in its efforts to protest against violence and institutional racism against black people.

In January 2017, millions of women across the world joined the Women's March for equality. The march organization is committed to the use of non-violent resistance to "dismantle systems of oppression". Groups such as this draw on the strength and diversity of women to work towards a better world for all.

YES TO AN EQUAL, DIVERSE, AND PEACEFUL WORLD!

In 2018, more than a million people took part in the second US Women's March.

See also: 144–145

Rigoberta Menchú

Born 1959

It is hard to imagine a more devastating childhood than the one endured by Rigoberta Menchú Tum in Guatemala, where her family members were tortured and killed by the government. But the horror of her experiences spurred her on to become a world-renowned activist for indigenous people. She works for peace, justice, and equality across the globe, encouraging and supporting other women to do the same.

> **"I am like a drop of water on a rock. After drip, drip, dripping in the same place, I begin to leave a mark..."**

to end the war. She also helped found an opposition group. In 1983, she attracted world attention through her memoir, *I, Rigoberta Menchú*, which described the abuse of civil rights in her country, especially against women. When the war ended, Menchú successfully fought for the military leaders to be brought to trial for human rights abuses.

Youth activist

During Guatemala's long civil war (1960–96), indigenous people were targeted by the elite who ruled the country by force. Herself part of the Mayan K'iche' ethnic group, Rigoberta Menchú Tum (often known just as Rigoberta Menchú), witnessed the struggle first-hand. Her parents and two brothers were murdered by the regime due to their activism.

Campaigning in exile

In 1981, after fleeing to Mexico, she joined international groups trying to put pressure on Guatemala's government

Nobel Peace Prize

In 1992, Menchú was awarded the Nobel Peace Prize in recognition of her work. In 2006, she established the Nobel Women Initiative with five other female Nobel Peace Prize laureates: Betty Williams (Ireland, 1976), Mairead Maguire (Northern Ireland, 1976), Jody Williams (US, 1997), Shirin Ebadi (Iran, 2003), and Wangari Maathai (Kenya, 2004). Since then, Leymah Gbowee (Liberia, 2011) and Tawakkol Karman (Yemen, 2011) have joined their initiative, which helps women across the world to improve their lives.

Nobel women
Through the Nobel Women's Initiative, Menchú has worked to support many grassroots movements around the world. She is seen here in 2017 protesting mining operations in Guatemala, together with Yemeni activist and fellow Nobel woman Tawakkol Karman.

Voting power
Dressed in traditional Mayan clothes, Rigoberta Menchú is pictured voting in the Guatemalan election of 2011. She ran as a presidential candidate, but was defeated in the first round.

A global FEMINISM

Do all women around the world wake up to the same reality and face the same challenges? We can all strive to be feminists, but when each woman's experience is different from every other's, is it possible to find a "one-size-fits-all" approach to feminism? Do we need to rethink what solidarity means?

Global sisterhood

The ideal of a "global sisterhood" was framed by some Western feminists, including American author and activist Robin Morgan, in the 1970s and 1980s. They hoped to roll out the social changes achieved in the US and Europe across the globe, but have since been criticized for ignoring the diversity of women's lives around the world. Other feminists said their brand of feminism applied mainly to white, middle-class, Western women. In her 2006 book *Pedagogies of Crossing* Afro-Caribbean feminist academic Jacqui

Alexander observes that while lots of women wake up in a warm home stocked with food, and school or work to go to, others face a very different reality. Many women may start their day tired, cold, hungry, and afraid. Feminism must account for these women, too.

US feminist academic Chandra Talpade Mohanty, herself originally from India, has further argued that feminism in the global north (generally richer countries) is sometimes portrayed as "saving" women in the global south. Her book *Feminism without Borders* (2003) suggests that many Western feminists still have a "colonial mindset" – treating all women from poorer countries as just one "other" oppressed class, while simultaneously ignoring the history of colonization by richer countries that caused problems for these women in the first place. Mohanty also sees Western feminists as too often measuring success along capitalist lines, and focusing on seeking financial equality for women. For her, a truly global feminism should go beyond trying to improve women's place within Western economic and political structures.

ONE BILLION RISING

Since its launch on Valentine's Day in 2012, One Billion Rising has brought people together around the world every 14th February to "RISE in defiance of the injustices women suffer, demanding an end at last to violence against women". The campaign is named for the one billion women who, statistically, will be beaten or raped during their lifetime.

A local approach

Many global feminist movements argue that feminism should examine not only the issues that affect women's lives globally, but also how they affect women in the places they live. For example, equality in education is an issue affecting young girls worldwide. But, while in Europe and the US feminists may focus on getting girls into subjects like STEM, in rural areas of India and

Nepal the issue may be getting girls into the classroom at all. The barriers facing these girls are different; they might not be able to go to school because they are on their period and there is a lack of facilities, or negative taboos surrounding this. In areas like these, the global goal of equal education for girls cannot succeed without addressing local provisions and cultural attitudes.

Crossing borders

In the era of globalization, women may also have multiple identities. Latina feminist Patricia Valoy, who lives in New York, USA, argues that Western feminist theory sometimes overstates gender as the cause of inequality, and "does not consider the ways in which women of color are oppressed along racial and class lines". Valoy instead backs the idea of transnational feminism, which seeks to "examine issues across nationality (including race and ethnicity), sex, gender, and class."

Working together

Overall, both Valoy and Mohanty suggest that solidarity cannot be achieved by viewing all women as a unified group. Feminism without borders does not mean ignoring the borders and differences between women around the world, but recognizing the challenges these differences present, and using localized strategies to achieve global goals.

> **"Diversity and difference are central values here – to be acknowledged and respected."**
>
> **Chandra Talpade Mohanty,**
> *Feminism without Borders* (2003)

MANY FACTORS INFLUENCE HOW WOMEN EXPERIENCE INEQUALITY AROUND THE WORLD

Can MEN be FEMINISTS?

Yes! To be a feminist is to believe in the equality of the genders. In the words of American writer bell hooks, "feminism is a movement to end sexism, sexist exploitation, and oppression". Feminism is for everyone regardless of gender, race, or class.

See also: 14–15, 114–115

Fighting for equality

Feminists have always had male allies. In 1817, English philosopher Jeremy Bentham (1748–1842) argued for the political freedom of women in his Plan of Parliamentary Reform. He later said that he saw no reason for women not to have suffrage, other than too many people being against it. He also argued for the use of the gender-neutral term "person" rather than "man" in his political writing. A generation later, another English philosopher, John Stuart Mill (1806–1873), advocated equality of the sexes alongside his wife Harriet Taylor Mill, whose radical essay "The Enfranchisement of Women" (1851) was published under his name. She argued that women should not live in "separate spheres" to men and should have full access to work outside the home.

Some people use "pro-feminist" rather than "feminist" to describe men who are allies to feminism.

I AM A FEMINIST!

AROUND THE WORLD, STAND TOGETHER FOR

"I am going to keep saying... that I am a feminist until it is met with a shrug."

Justin Trudeau, Canadian Prime Minister (2016)

Male allies

Today, the #HeForShe initiative by the UN Women organization encourages men and boys to be involved in the campaign for gender equality. Men in politics who have advocated for women's rights include former US President Barack Obama. In a 2016 interview with *Glamour* magazine, Obama quoted UK campaign group the Fawcett Society's slogan, "This Is What a Feminist Looks Like"

WHITE RIBBON CAMPAIGN

The White Ribbon Campaign was set up in Canada in 1991 to encourage an end to male violence against women once and for all. They argue that men and boys must work together in "calling out violent, bullying behaviour amongst their peers, and spreading a message of equality and respect". The campaign has spread to more than 60 countries.

and spoke about the positive consequences for everyone of improving girls' and women's lives. Obama also helped launch the It's On Us campaign to end sexual assault, which promoted the message that it is the responsibility of everyone to take a stand against violence.

Feminists or allies?

Some feminists – and some men - feel that men should not identify as feminists. This is mainly because they believe that feminism is a movement for and by women, and that men are not able to opt out of the privileges of a patriarchal society. Other feminists think that while most men may be disturbed by a culture of patriarchy in which, as bell hooks writes, men "are required to dominate women, to exploit, and oppress us", they may fear letting go of the privilege it affords them. However, organizations such as the New York-based A Call To Men believe that it is only by redefining what manhood means that we will create a better world for girls and women. A Call to Men creates partnerships with groups, both nationally and locally, such as in schools, universities, businesses, local government, sports, and the military, to change sexist attitudes towards women and girls.

Acknowledgements

Dorling Kindersley would like to thank Ann Baggaley for editorial assistance, Gregory McCarthy for design assistance, Carron Brown for proofreading and for the index, and Professor Chris Frith for reviewing pp 50–51.

The publisher would like to thank the following for their kind permission to reproduce their photographs:

(Key: a–above; b–below/bottom; c–center; f–far; l–left; r–right; t–top)

2 Library of Congress, Washington, D.C.: LC-USZ62-75334. **10 Alamy Stock Photo:** Niday Picture Library. **14 Alamy Stock Photo:** Granger Historical Picture Archive (bc). **17 Getty Images:** FPG (tr). **18 Library of Congress, Washington, D.C.:** LC-USZ62-7816 (bc). **20 Getty Images:** Library of Congress (cr). **21 Library of Congress, Washington, D.C.:** LC-DIG-ppmsca-52069. **24 Getty Images:** Hulton Deutsch (cr). **25 Getty Images:** Jimmy Sime. **27 Getty Images:** TASS (tr). **28 Alamy Stock Photo:** Vadim Rodnev (bl). **31 Getty Images:** Bettmann (br). **32 Reprinted by permission of Ms. magazine:** © 1972 (cr). **33 Getty Images:** Yale Joel. **35 Bridgeman Images:** © Rene Saint Paul (br). **36 iStockphoto.com:** stray_cat (bl). **39 Getty Images:** Images Press (tr). **41 Alamy Stock Photo:** Stockbroker (bl). **43 Alamy Stock Photo:** Doreen Kennedy (tr). **44 Getty Images:** Stuart C. Wilson (cr). **45 Getty Images:** Michael Loccisano. **46 Alamy Stock Photo:** Image Source. **49 Getty Images:** Luis Acosta (cr). **51 Alamy Stock Photo:** Peter Cavanagh (cr). **53 Loulou d'Aki:** (tr). **54 Getty Images:** Jean Tesseyre (cr). **55 Getty Images:** Roger Viollet Collection. **56 Getty Images:** Jerod Harris (br). **59 Getty Images:** Tibrina Hobson (tr). **60 Alamy Stock Photo:** Don Smetzer (cr). **61 Courtesy of bell hooks Institute. 63 Getty Images:** David M. Benett (br). **64 Depositphotos Inc:** tungphoto. **66 Getty Images:** Chris Tobin (bl). **68 Getty Images:** Paul Morigi (bl). **71 Getty Images:** Justin Sullivan (bl). **72 Dorling Kindersley:** used with permission of Judith Butler (cr). **73 Judith Butler:** Stefan Gutermuth.

75 Dreamstime.com: Volodymyr Ivash (tr). **77 Getty Images:** Fred W. McDarrah (br). **79 Alamy Stock Photo:** Emma Kim / Cultura RM (cr). **81 Alamy Stock Photo:** Graham Oliver (br). **83 Getty Images:** Sam Panthaky / AFP (tr). **84 Alamy Stock Photo:** Michael Preston (br). **86 Alamy Stock Photo:** Pictorial Press Ltd (cr). **87 Alamy Stock Photo:** Archivart / © Banco de México Diego Rivera Frida Kahlo Museums Trust, Mexico, D.F. / © DACS 2018. **88 Reuters:** Katy Migiro (bl). **90 Getty Images:** Martin Bernetti / AFP (bl). **93 Alamy Stock Photo:** Janine Wiedel Photolibrary (br). **94 Alamy Stock Photo:** Picade LLC. **97 Alamy Stock Photo:** Photononstop (cr). **98 The Orion Publishing Group Ltd.:** Cover of 'I am Malala' by Malala Yousafzai (cr). **99 Getty Images:** Tony Karumba / AFP. **101 Getty Images:** Godong (tr). **102 Alamy Stock Photo:** Hero Images Inc. (bl). **104 Getty Images:** Grant Lamos IV (cr). **105 Getty Images:** Robert Alexander. **106 Getty Images:** Alfred Eisenstaedt / The LIFE Picture Collection (bl). **109 Alamy Stock Photo:** Granger Historical Picture Archive (tr). **111 Getty Images:** Herve Gloaguen (bl). **113 Dreamstime.com:** Monkey Business Images (cr). **114 Rex by Shutterstock:** Felipe Trueba / EPA-EFE (bl). **116 Getty Images:** The Asahi Shimbun. **119 Getty Images:** PhotoAlto / Frederic Cirou (cr). **121 Getty Images:** Tristan Fewings (tr). **122 Alamy Stock Photo:** Richard Levine (bl). **125 Bridgeman Images:** Royal Collection Trust © Her Majesty Queen Elizabeth II, 2018 (tr). **127 Getty Images:** Ute Grabowsky (tr). **129 courtesy of gal-dem. 130 Alamy Stock Photo:** Lev Dolgachov (br). **133 Rex by Shutterstock:** Les Wilson (tr). **135 Alamy Stock Photo:** Angela Hampton Picture Library (tr). **136 www.emma.de:** (cr). **137 Getty Images:** ullstein bild. **139 Getty Images:** Adam Berry (cr). **141 Rex by Shutterstock:** Eduardo DiBaia / AP (tr). **142 Getty Images:** Johan Ordonez / AFP (cr). **143 Getty Images:** Orlando Sierra / AFP. **144 Getty Images:** Noel Celis / AFP (bl). **147 Getty Images:** Hannah Peters (cr)

All other images © Dorling Kindersley
For further information see: www.dkimages.com